The Wellness Principles

by Gary Deng, MD, PhD

The Wellness Principles

Cooking for a Healthy Life
by Gary Deng, MD, PhD

Legend

(V)   Vegetarian

(VEGAN)   Vegan

    Nut-free

    Dairy-free

    Gluten-free

(<5)   5 ingredients or fewer

(30)   30 minutes or less

How to Eat Well, Live Well, Stay Well

"What should I eat?"

Over the past twenty years, I have been asked this question by thousands of patients in my medical practice. To me, this question should be asked before one gets sick, because proper nutrition strengthens the body and can prevent many diseases. In fact, the most common illnesses in modern society—such as cardiovascular disease, diabetes, and cancers—can be related to our behaviors and lifestyle, including what and how we eat. There are a lot of things in life that we cannot change, but we can change our diet and lifestyle if we make a conscious effort. And such changes should happen as early as possible, but it's never too late.

In the early part of my medical career, I was frustrated to see how we could treat patients with a chronic medical problem, make them better, and discharge them from the hospital, only to have them readmitted for the same problem not long afterward. For example, there were patients admitted for lung illness requiring respiratory support, yet they continued to smoke after their release and fell ill again soon after. There were patients admitted for a heart attack, had coronary artery stents put in, yet continued to eat buttery steaks and French fries regularly, then had another cardiac event. I felt as if we were often putting out fires, temporarily tidying up a cluttered house that still had tinder and burning candles everywhere.

Without day-to-day health maintenance, the human body will deteriorate as we get older and reach one breaking point after another. So I started to guide patients on their wellness outside the hospital and in between clinic visits, outlining self-care practices that would nurture their health—both healthy eating and healthy living. It was satisfying when I saw how much my patients both appreciated and benefited from this approach, and how it improved their health and life in general.

Many of us are restrained to various degrees by time, energy, and finances. We know it's best to eat tasty, nutritious, and healthy foods made of fresh, quality ingredients. And when it's home-cooked, we have greater control over what goes into the meal, and it is often less expensive than eating out. It's a dilemma ... You can get delicious and healthy food at a nice restaurant, but that can be expensive. You can get inexpensive and tasty fast or prepared food, but these meals are not always very healthy. Or you can prepare a nutritious meal at home at reasonable cost, but it takes time that you don't have. One of the main reasons I wrote this book is to help busy people prepare healthy and tasty meals at home quickly, so it's achievable most of the time. These are the recipes I cook for my family almost every day.

In addition to the recipes, I explain basic healthy eating principles based on scientific evidence and how to incorporate these into daily life. Each recipe uses healthy ingredients—plant oils instead of butter, very small amounts of sugar, and less salt than typical recipes. They are heavy on fresh vegetables, whole grains, and seafood, although there are a few meat dishes for a change of pace from time to time. The proportion of vegetables on the plate might be of a larger quantity than usual. There are no desserts made from refined flour in the traditional sense; instead, the recipes feature fruits and nuts with little added sugar, taking advantage of the sweetness offered by the ingredients themselves. I also use healthy cooking methods such as sautéing, baking, boiling, and steaming to get the maximum nutritious benefits from the ingredients. The recipes, pairing suggestions, and even food shopping strategies emphasize the balance of macronutrients and complexity and diversity of micronutrients. Sample menus are listed at the back of the book.

To make meals tasty, each recipe starts with high-quality ingredients. If the ingredients are fresh, you can do minimal cooking and the dish will still be delicious. There are tips on how to select quality ingredients, plus information on how flavors are generated and how to use that knowledge to naturally enhance the taste of a dish.

To make meal preparation quick, most dishes are designed to be completed in thirty minutes. Those that require more time are structured to minimize hands-on time, by using slow-cooking methods that require little attention. Although "mise en place"—having all your ingredients prepared and ready before cooking—is the preferred method, some recipes in this book interlace prepping and cooking to save time.

There is a lot of confusion out there about diet: One source may rave about certain foods being healthy while another may dismiss their value or even discourage eating those same foods. Some dietary advice is so strict that it is almost impossible to follow long term. We need to put things in perspective. In this book, I will talk about what really matters and what doesn't, hoping to clear up some confusion about diet and nutrition.

In addition to healthy eating, optimal health depends on many other lifestyle aspects, such as physical exercise, stress management, sleep, circadian rhythms, social support, and elements that nurture our mind, body, and spirit. Without them, you can eat healthy yet still lack physical and mental resilience. I will therefore look at the principles of health "beyond the plate."

My own interest in food began when I was a teenager, after reading a novel about the life of a food connoisseur.

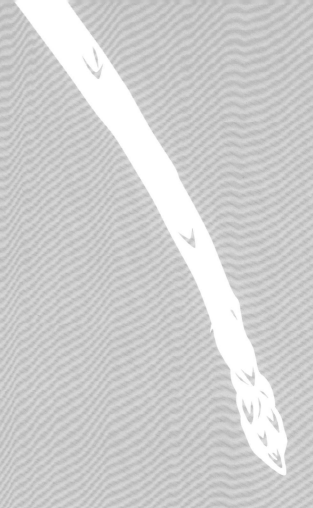

I was amazed to find that there was so much enjoyment, beauty, and intricacy to be found in eating well, and not just to fill our stomachs. I had discovered the culinary arts. Later, when doing experiments in molecular biology while working on my PhD—cloning genes and studying viruses and cancer-fighting immune cells—my mentor told me that "Our work is like cooking. Both are chemical reactions. Just follow the recipes." And so I discovered the culinary sciences as well. My interest was piqued, and I wanted to learn more, so my actual home cooking started quite late in life. But as with everything else, once you have a passion for something, it is no longer a burden. The time I spend cooking is fun for me. And the more I enjoyed it, the more thought and heart I put into it, the better I became at it, and so my cooking improved.

I would like to share with you my life experience, culinary explorations, and professional expertise in basic biological science and clinical medicine, incorporating Western and Eastern health philosophies and practices. I hope this book becomes a useful guide in your quest for better health, and brings you and your family culinary delights. Together we can cook our way toward optimal health and wellness—eat well, live well, and stay well.

Healthy Eating Principles

Our health is influenced to a large degree by our diet. What we eat and how we eat has a global effect on our body. Every cell is exposed to the biochemical and metabolic environment created by our diet. If we eat healthy foods, the nutrients enhance the function of the cells. If we eat unhealthy foods, the harmful substances hurt and stress the cells, making them malfunction, age faster, or even mutate. Food for our body is like fuel for a car. If we put clean fuel into a car, the engine will run better and last longer. If we use fuel contaminated with water or dirt, the engine will not run effectively and will break down sooner.

Most of us already know that our overall health depends on a healthy diet. We know which foods are good for us and which are not so good. But how to maintain a long-term healthy diet and also make meals that are tasty is the challenge. And meeting that challenge is why I wrote this book. Let's start with the core healthy eating principles.

Plant-Based Eating

Dietary trends change from year to year, and it can get confusing, however the consensus in the medical and scientific worlds is that a plant-based approach is the common denominator of a healthy diet.

The "plant" here refers to vegetables, fruits, legumes, nuts, seeds, and grains. Plant-"based" means that the majority of what we eat comes from plant products. It can be but doesn't have to be vegan (no animal products at all) or vegetarian (egg and dairy products allowed)—both of these diets are very healthy but may not be easy to follow or are impractical for a lot of people. You can view a plant-based diet as a vegan diet plus select high-quality animal proteins such as fish, shellfish, and eggs, with occasional poultry and meat.

Specifically, I recommend eating meat no more than two times a week, poultry no more than three times a week, fish and shellfish 2–5 times a week, and eggs 3–6 times a week, with a total of no more than 14 servings of animal protein a week. The rest of your diet should ideally come from plants. This means that of your three meals each day, one is ideally vegan and the other two would have one serving each of animal protein.

By the same token, I use a plant-based oil when cooking, such as olive oil, canola (rapeseed) oil, or other seed oils, rather than butter, bacon fat, or lard. If a dish calls for the use of butter for flavor, use ½ tablespoon instead of the "3 tablespoons" that we sometimes see in recipes. The same goes for cheese, which is very flavorful and can give a dish that savory umami taste. But just use a few gratings or small chunks, rather than several ounces or cups of cheese—just enough to make the dish interesting, rather than as a significant source of protein. Try using mushrooms and tomatoes instead to achieve a similar umami taste.

In this book, you will find that the ingredients and composition of most meals adhere to this principle. The serving size of vegetables is usually larger than in other recipes, and the serving sizes of proteins and carbohydrates are smaller. When putting together a meal with a meat dish, balance it with plenty of vegetables in a ratio of roughly one meat serving paired with two vegetable servings.

A plant-based diet is not a strict, draconian, and restrictive diet. It offers some flexibility, so that following it doesn't become a source of stress. Not being able to stick to it 100 percent should not become a source of guilt either.

If you can't follow a diet long term, you can't reap the long-term benefits. For example, cutting out red meat or sugar completely can be nearly impossible for some people, and they give up or feel guilty every time they eat a steak or ice cream. However, occasional splurges are fine because the effect of diet on the body is long term and cumulative, based on average exposure to the foods over years, if not decades. Biological effects are dose-dependent; it is what you eat regularly that matters. We want to enjoy our food, as well as eat healthy.

Eating a Balanced Diet

Our bodies need macronutrients and micronutrients to function properly. Macronutrients are those nutrients we need in large amounts, such as carbohydrates, proteins, fats, fiber, electrolytes, and water. Micronutrients are elements we need only in small amounts, such as minerals, vitamins, and other substances that make cells function better, including iron, zinc, iodine, co-enzymes, antioxidants, and flavonoids. Eating the ideal ratio of macronutrients from each category, and the ideal amounts, in a meal are important for a healthy diet.

Carbohydrates

The main function of carbohydrates is to provide energy for our body. They are the fuel that keeps cellular activities going, and we need them to sustain life. Carbohydrates come in the form of starch and sugar. Starch is sugar molecules strung together; if starch is a pearl necklace, sugar is the pearl. In some foods, carbohydrates exist as starch, such as bread, rice, pasta, other grains, potatoes, and sweet potatoes. All digestible starch foods are converted to sugar in the body to be absorbed. In other foods, such as fruits, carbohydrates exist mainly as sugar, which needs no digestion to be absorbed. Ultimately, all starch and sugar are converted to glucose, which is the form of sugar the cells can use directly as fuel.

The Glycemic Index (GI) measures how fast carbo-hydrates are converted to glucose in the body—the higher the number, the faster a starchy food raises the glucose level in the blood. For example, white rice has a GI of 70–80, whereas brown rice is 40–50. White bread is in the 70s and pasta or whole-wheat bread in the 50s. Foods with a GI higher than 70 are considered high-GI foods, and you should eat less of those. From 56 to 69 are considered medium (don't eat too much). Those below 55 are low (less concerns of raising blood sugar levels).

When we don't eat enough carbohydrates, our bodies will convert fat and protein to usable fuels, but that process is not as quick and efficient as converting carbohydrates. This is where a low-carbohydrate diet can help in losing weight. When we eat more carbohydrates than we need—quite easy in modern society—the body converts excess energy to fat, as stored energy for rainy days, leading to weight gain. To maintain a healthy weight, we need just the right balance of carbohydrates in our diet.

Proteins

Proteins form the structure of our body. If carbohydrates are the firewood that burns and keeps the house warm, proteins are the bricks and mortar that make the house stand. Proteins are also strings of pearls, with each pearl an amino acid. There are twenty different amino acids, so imagine twenty different colors of pearl. The body needs to get the right balance of these amino acids from foods, and we need to eat a variety of protein-rich foods to achieve the proper balance. For example, many plant proteins do not have the ideal balance of amino acids by themselves. Thus, pairing with other plant proteins and supplementing with animal proteins is important. Adults don't need a lot of protein, unless you are a bodybuilder or recovering from an illness. Protein can also be used as fuel for the body, but it doesn't create the glucose spike in the blood in the same way as carbohydrates, reducing the harm to the body from exposure to excessive sugar while providing the same amount of energy.

Fats

Fats are mainly used by the body as storage energy in the form of triglycerides. This is densely packed energy, more than twice as dense by weight as carbohydrates. Think about it as the garage, attic, or storage room. When we have more stuff than we need, we put it there for future use. When we are running short, we take it out. This makes a lot of sense, since throughout human history, most people didn't have a constant food supply, so when there was food, people would eat as much as they could in order to store the excess. In our day and age, food is more abundant and accessible, and it is too easy to eat more than we need.

When using fats in cooking, those from an animal source, such as butter, lard, and tallow are high in saturated fat—not so good for health. Plant oils are better: Olive oil, sunflower seed oil, safflower oil, canola (rapeseed) oil, and avocado oil are all high in monounsaturated fat, a particular healthy type of fat. Avocado oil has the added advantage of having a higher smoke point (about 480°F/250°C) than olive oil (about 375°F/190°C), so can be used when high-temperature searing is needed.

Fiber

Fiber is indigestible carbohydrate that influences the movement of foods through the digestive tract and cultivates the microbiota in our gut. High fiber intake has been associated with lower risk of diabetes, cardiovascular diseases, and certain types of cancer. Fiber comes from vegetables, fruits, legumes, seeds, and whole grains. Each of those foods contains a mix of different subtypes of fiber, each acting differently on our digestive tract. To get the most benefits, we need to eat a large variety of fiber-rich foods.

Electrolytes

The major electrolytes the body needs and gets from foods are sodium, potassium, magnesium, and calcium. Every food has a little bit of each, although the composition differs from food to food. The body has an amazing ability to maintain a stable level of electrolytes. If there is not enough in our diet, the body will hold on to what we already have. If there is too much, the body will eliminate them, mostly through the kidneys. When electrolytes are out of balance, we may develop cramps, weakness, or even cardiac arrhythmia. When we don't have enough electrolytes, we cannot hold water in our bloodstream and we get dehydrated, even when we drink plenty of water. (In this case, drink some broth or add a pinch of salt to your beverages.) This is why, for example, runners always drink water with some electrolytes in it as opposed to plain water. Most foods have some electrolytes in them and if we eat a variety of foods in moderation, we usually get enough.

Water

Water is an often overlooked macronutrient. But water is essential to life. It is also the best detoxifier; keeping ourselves well hydrated at all times will help flush the toxins and waste out of our systems as quickly as possible. Don't wait to drink water until you feel thirsty. The brain senses thirst only when the body has already lost enough water to become somewhat dehydrated. Becoming thirsty and then drinking a large amount creates a wide fluctuation in our state of hydration and the body doesn't like it. The eight glasses of water we are supposed to drink every day should be sipped throughout the day, not chugged down a whole glass at a time. This keeps a stable amount of water in our circulation. You can add a wedge of lemon or lime to give it a more refreshing taste, if needed, and always drink room-temperature water, as cold water chills the stomach and can make our digestive functions sluggish.

Soft drinks and fruit juices contain too much sugar, and even diet soft drinks have been shown to lead to weight gain because of the effect of the sense of "sweetness"

on the brain. Coffee or tea is fine in small amounts, if followed by water, although they do have a diuretic effect. Soups and broths are also good because they contain electrolytes, which hold water in the blood vessels, although again they do need to be followed by drinking water as well, because the body needs more water than electrolytes.

Now that we understand each category of macronutrients, it is clear we need all of them. But we can only eat so much in a day, so the ratio of the macronutrients is important. Eating too much of one category can cause a shortage in others. The best diet gives us the proper proportion of these nutrients.

Portion and Proportion

For most people, the ideal proportion of nutrients is a 2:1:1 ratio. Two parts vegetables and fruits, one part proteins, and one part carbohydrates. If you look at your plate, one half should be vegetables and fruits, one quarter proteins, and one quarter carbohydrates, with some plant-based fat (oil) mixed in here and there. This is probably different from what you are used to in a restaurant meal, where the proteins or carbohydrates are the main dish and the vegetables are in a smaller portion served on the side.

When composing a complete meal, keep this 2:1:1 ratio in mind. In this book, most recipes are either a vegetable dish, a protein dish, or a carbohydrate dish. If you have decided on a protein dish as the main component of a meal, pair it with a carbohydrate-rich dish of roughly equal proportion and twice the quantity of vegetables and fruits—try not to overdo fruits however, because of their sugar content (page 18). If you have decided on a vegetable dish as the main component, pair it with

another vegetable dish, a protein dish, and a carbohydrate dish. I have given pairing suggestions for each recipe, based on how much of each macronutrient is in that dish. Some dishes contain more than one macronutrient in a substantial way, and the pairing suggestions keep that in mind. For example, if a dish contains both proteins and vegetables, I would note that it only needs to pair with another vegetable dish and a carbohydrate dish. A few recipes have all the macronutrients, making them a one-pot meal, with perhaps the addition of a vegetable dish, if called for. Just follow the pairing suggestions and you will have balanced, complete meals.

Fats/oils are usually combined with the protein, carbohydrates, and vegetables. So they are not included in the 2:1:1 ratio. We should include roughly 60–90 grams of fat a day for a 2:1:1 dietary proportion. That is the equivalent of 1–2 tablespoons of olive oil per meal. For a low-carbohydrate diet, more fat can be incorporated into the dishes to make up the shortfall in calories and make you feel full while eating less food—about 120 grams of fat a day, equivalent to 2–3 tablespoons of olive oil per meal.

Portion size is very important. I suggest you follow the "70 percent full" rule. Eat slowly, then once you don't feel hungry anymore (usually around 50 percent full), eat just a little more and stop. Don't eat all the way to 100 percent full, which tends to lead to an excess of nutrients and weight gain. We may have an instant satisfaction, but we are undermining our long-term health.

Since we don't always have time to measure everything, using one's fist is a quick way to estimate portion size. For a meal, one-quarter of the plate should be about the size of our fist. If you are a large person, the fist is bigger and you eat more. A smaller person eats less. In the 2:1:1 ratio scenario, one would eat a fist-size portion of carbohydrates (perhaps a small dinner roll or small bowl of rice), another fist-size portion of proteins (could be a small bowl of beans or 6–8 ounces of salmon) and two fist-size portions of vegetables (cooked and packed down). If the vegetable dish is a leafy salad, measure it packed down (compressed), not loose.

Ideally, each of the three meals of the day should have this portion and proportion. Too often we eat a quick and small breakfast (perhaps 10 percent of our daily intake), a hurried cold lunch (about 20 percent), and a large, satisfying dinner (about 70 percent). Generally, we don't do much after dinner and don't expend much energy, so all that excess caloric intake has nowhere to go but be converted to fat, leading to weight gain.

Equally important is when you eat dinner. If you eat a large dinner close to bedtime, it doesn't allow time for the food to digest efficiently and it prevents us from sleeping soundly. We should try to fit our caloric intake into a schedule of an eleven-hour period. If we eat breakfast around 8 a.m., we should finish dinner by 7 p.m. With this in mind, we should eat about 30 percent of our daily intake at breakfast, 40 percent at lunch, and 30 percent at an early dinner. A recent study showed that people lose more weight if they eat a large breakfast instead of a large dinner, even when the total amount of calories they eat in a day is the same.

Complexity of Ingredients

In addition to the macronutrients, our body needs many micronutrients to stay in top shape and function at top level. There are thousands of biochemical reactions happening in our bodies at any given moment. For example, converting glucose to something more usable by the cells takes ten steps of chemical reaction, all of which are influenced by the presence or absence of many chemicals.

A complex diet will provide such diversity and contribute to our health. Each food has its own nutrient profile, and we need to eat different foods to get the benefit of the sum of their profiles. For example, broccoli may be good, but if you eat broccoli as the vegetable in every meal, you will miss out on what other vegetables have to offer. Some foods are high in iron, some in calcium, others in zinc. Our body needs all of them. And this complexity forms part of our balanced diet. Every good nutrient can turn into a bad nutrient if we eat too much of it. For example, our body needs iron, calcium, and B6, but taking in too much isn't good for us either. Here is how to achieve complexity in our diet:

1. Use fresh ingredients.
   Fresh foods have the most nutrients. As ingredients sit on a shelf or in a refrigerator, they slowly lose nutrients by degradation or evaporation. When shopping, go for the freshest ingredients and buy foods in season. Farmers' markets are good places to shop because the produce is usually harvested the day before. How do we know whether food is fresh or not? Smell it! Fresh produce is very fragrant, and fresh seafood doesn't have a "fishy" odor. Try smelling a freshly picked apple, tomato, or carrot, then smell the one that has been sitting around on your kitchen table or a supermarket shelf for several days—you will notice the difference. Fragrance is the first thing to dissipate after produce is harvested. Even fresh grains such as wheat or rice have a special fragrance. With industrialization of our food supply, it is increasingly difficult to get truly fresh ingredients. Sometimes it makes more sense to buy

frozen vegetables than vegetables on a store shelf, because the frozen ones are usually cleaned and frozen shortly after harvesting, preserving more nutrients.

2. Buy a variety of ingredients.
   When shopping for groceries, buy a wide variety of different items in small amounts, instead of a large amount of only a few items. For example, instead of buying lots of lettuce greens and tomatoes, buy a variety of salad greens (kale, spinach, etc.), tomatoes, beets (beetroot), bell peppers, cucumbers, zucchini (courgette), and eggplant (aubergine). Instead of just oats, buy other grains to make hot cereal for breakfast. Shopping this way is not more expensive. It just takes a bit of awareness and planning. On page 14, there are suggestions for how to stock a pantry.

3. Cook at home.
   With home cooking, you have total control of what you put in a dish. You can use high-quality, healthy ingredients, and a large variety of them, which may not be possible in an average restaurant meal. When shopping for groceries, try to avoid pre-made or boxed/canned foods. For example, dried beans are preferable to canned; with some planning, you can soak the beans in the morning, then you only need 30 minutes (with

5 minutes actual hands-on time) to cook them for dinner. In addition, home cooking makes economic sense. Nice restaurants use top-quality ingredients and sophisticated cooking processes so can be very expensive. For the same expense as dining in an average restaurant, you can buy very high-quality ingredients and make really tasty and healthy foods at home.

4. Eat a variety of dishes over a week.
   Change your menu from day to day, even though this may seem like a burden. With a little planning, and choosing meals that require only limited hands-on time, it is achievable. On page 248 there is a two-week sample menu as a guide to how to organize a complex and diverse diet. It was designed for those with a busy lifestyle, sometimes using leftovers for lunch and breakfast. Freshly made lunches can be made in the morning, using recipes that are "30 minutes or less." Planned this way, you can eat healthy meals for two weeks with only a few repeated dishes.

By eating a complex diet, we avoid having too much of one nutrient while coming up short on another, hence achieving the balance that will keep the body the healthiest. It is about moderation—a little bit of this and that, but not too much of anything. Spanish tapas dishes and Japanese bento boxes are good examples.

Complexity and balance also help us beyond a purely nutritional aspect. They make our whole approach to food more relaxed. When we eat a diverse diet, even an occasional "unhealthy" food won't hurt us much because it is balanced by a majority of good foods. Remember, the effect of nutrients on the body depends on the long-term exposure to those nutrients. Eating well occasionally won't do you much good, but if you eat well most of the time, an occasional lapse won't do you much harm. Unhealthy foods are not poisonous in the sense that they have an immediate harmful effect; it is the habit of eating them too regularly that is problematic.

By practicing complexity and balance in our diet, we achieve not only balance in nutrition, but also balance in mind. Focus on the big things and let the little things go.

Mindful Eating

Mindful eating means you are fully present in the moment. Your mind is with the food and the eating experience, not somewhere else—like the things you need to do that afternoon or what you wish you hadn't done yesterday. You shouldn't be eating while watching TV, reading, or emailing, even when alone.

The first level of mindful eating is to be aware of the food and its effect on the body. Is this food fresh and nutritious? Is the meal balanced and complex? Is it of the right portion and proportion? If not, maybe I should eat something else or add another ingredient or dish. The bottom line: Is this food making me healthier or less healthy?

The second level is to pay full attention to the food during the eating process. When you eat, look at the food, appreciate its visual beauty. Before you put it in your mouth, smell it. Try to discern the complexity of the fragrance and appreciate it. After putting it in your mouth, chew slowly, ten times or more. Break up the pieces and release the locked flavors. Feel the texture changing in your mouth. After swallowing, experience the aftertaste. At lower concentrations, the fragrances and flavors take on a different character, sometimes even better than when you first put the food in your mouth. Experience the differences.

A third level of mindful eating is to be aware of how your body feels when eating. Are you actually hungry? Don't rush or cave in to the urge to satisfy that hunger quickly. Even when you slow down, the food will still be there in front of you. If you eat too quickly, the stomach may be full yet the brain still tells the body to eat more, because the nutrients haven't been absorbed and sent to the brain to tell you that you've had enough—and you end up overeating. And just because a food is delicious doesn't mean you should fill yourself to the brim. If you are about 70 percent full, you should stop eating.

These three levels are useful because the mind has a powerful effect on how the body functions. When your mind is focused on the food you are eating, the brain sends signals to all parts of the digestive system to make them ready to digest and absorb nutrients. The body also sends signals to the brain, telling it how it feels. Our body usually tells us what it does and doesn't need, if we care to listen.

Of course, there are times when this level of mindfulness may not seem possible. For example, at a work lunch where you want to chat with colleagues, or at a family dinner when everyone is reporting how their day went. Even on those occasions, try to find a moment to pause and comment on the foods as part of the conversation. You can be chewing and appreciating the food while quietly listening to what other people have to say. In those cases where it is impossible to practice completely mindful eating, don't sweat it. Just go with the flow and do it with your next meal.

This deliberate process may initially appear too elaborate, but after practicing it for a while, it will become an easy habit. You will see you are eating healthier and extracting the most out of the foods you consume, both in nutrients and enjoyment.

How to Stock a Pantry

One of the secrets to adhering to healthy eating principles is in grocery shopping and stocking your pantry. Buy a large variety of ingredients, each in a small amount. For example, instead of one big bag of all-purpose (plain) flour and one big bag of white rice, buy small bags of a variety of whole grains. Instead of a large bag of apples and a large bag of oranges, buy a few apples and oranges, a few boxes of berries, some pears, some kiwis, a couple mangoes, and a bunch of bananas. In this section, I'll explain in more detail how to shop for each category of ingredients.

Dry Goods

Grains
Grains make up the carbohydrate portion of our dishes. Buy mostly whole grains, which have a lower glycemic index (page 9), with a small amount of refined grains for those dishes that need them. Once the bags are opened, the contents should be used within a few weeks.

For longer storage, put the grains in sealed containers (glass is preferable to plastic). Ideally, when you open the door of your pantry, you should see a lineup of jars with five to ten different kinds of whole grains.

Barley: Whole barley berries to make soups or for salads.

Buckwheat: Crushed buckwheat groats (to make kasha) and soba noodles. (Like quinoa below, buckwheat is not a true grain, but is so nutritionally similar that it is treated as such.)

Corn: Coarse and fine whole-grain cornmeal to make grits and polenta, and a small amount of cornstarch (cornflour) to coat certain ingredients to develop a crust.

Millet: Both small and large millet, which have different textures and flavors.

Oats: Oat groats (whole oats), steel-cut (Scotch) oats, and rolled oats. Each provides a different texture.

Quinoa: Both white and red or black quinoa. When cooked, white quinoa is fluffy and has a mild taste. Red and black quinoa hold their shape better when cooked, are crunchier, and have a nuttier taste.

Rice: Both short-grain and long-grain brown rice, as well as black and wild rices. And small amounts of short- and long-grain white rice, and sweet rice (also known as glutinous or sticky) for occasional use to create certain textures.

Wheat: Instead of all-purpose (plain) bleached white flour, buy whole-wheat flour, farro berries (an ancient wheat grain), freekeh (roasted green durum wheat, also known as *farik*), and bulgur and pasta made of durum wheat (which has a lower glycemic index than whole-wheat bread, despite not being whole wheat).

Nuts and Seeds
These are a good source of plant-based protein, and are also rich in plant-based oils. When toasted, they produce fragrance and flavor that will enhance a dish. Buy small batches, store in sealed containers, and use them quickly to prevent oxidation of their fatty acids, which produces a stale and rancid taste. Keep small bags of a few different kinds in your freezer for longer storage.

Branch out beyond peanuts and eat more tree nuts, such as almonds, pecans, walnuts, cashews, Brazil nuts, pistachios, macadamia nuts, and hazelnuts. Grass seeds, such as flaxseeds, chia seeds, sesame seeds, pumpkin seeds, and sunflower seeds have special fatty acids and/ or unique flavors. They are a great addition to smoothies, breakfast cereals, and salads.

figs have a higher glycemic index, so I only use them on occasion. I would put chocolate chips or chunks in this category because they can be used the same way.

Keep a small amount of sun-dried tomatoes to add color and umami to some main dishes. Dried goji berries can also be used in soups, salads, and cooked dishes, and they are wonderfully colorful.

Room Temperature

Oils, Vinegars, Wines, and Sauces

Keep the following four types of cooking oil on hand: a large bottle of regular olive oil for general cooking, a small bottle of high-quality extra-virgin olive oil for when you need to add a fresh finish to a dish, a small bottle of canola (rapeseed) oil for when you want a flavorless oil, and a small bottle of avocado oil for those occasional dishes when you need a high-temperature sear with a very high smoke point. You can also keep a small bottle of truffle oil and toasted sesame oil on hand—a dash of these adds flavor and interest to a dish.

Stock four kinds of vinegar as well: a large bottle of apple cider vinegar for general use, a small bottle of balsamic vinegar for salads and dishes that will benefit from its intense and complex flavor, a small bottle of distilled white vinegar for dishes where you need only acidity and no other flavor, and a small bottle of white wine or rice vinegar for dishes that need a milder flavor.

Keep three kinds of cooking wine available for everyday cooking: a dry white table wine (Pinot Gris or Sauvignon Blanc); a light rice wine (cooking sake); and a fortified wine such as sherry, Marsala, or Madeira. Occasionally a dish calls for triple sec (for its orange flavor), red table wine, or dark rice wine, but you don't need those on hand regularly.

For special flavors, stock one or several of these: light soy sauce (may not be gluten-free), tamari (usually gluten-free), mirin, hot sauce, fish sauce, Worcestershire sauce, and oyster sauce (best kept refrigerated).

Salt, Sugar, Spices, and Dried Herbs

Keep three kinds of salt on hand: Kosher (flaked) salt for when only clean saltiness is needed, such as in a dish that already has lots of flavor, or when dry-brining fish or meat since its flakiness extracts moisture better. Sea salt for when a bit of complexity is needed in the saltiness. Use fine sea salt when you need the salt quickly blended into the dish, such as right before a stew or soup is served, and coarse sea salt when you want to feel the distinct salty particles, such as in salad, fish, or vegetable dishes.

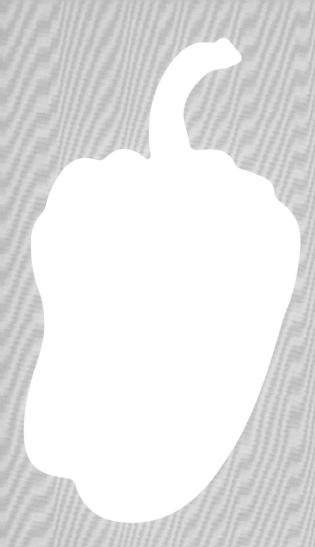

Legumes

Stock mostly dried beans, which have a better texture, more flavor, and more nutrients than canned beans. They are also a lot cheaper. Soak them overnight or for a few hours before cooking. Do also keep one or two cans of beans on hand for situations when you haven't planned ahead and want to make a bean dish in a hurry.

Keep some chickpeas, red kidney beans, white kidney beans (cannellini beans), pinto beans, black-eyed peas (black-eyed beans), fava beans (broad beans), lima beans (butter beans), lupini beans, adzuki beans, mung beans, soybeans, green lentils, red lentils, and urad lentils. They are full of plant-based protein and fiber—they also look great lined up in clear glass jars in your pantry.

Dried Fruits

Keep an assortment of dried fruits to use in breakfast cereals, yogurt cups, salads, and desserts. The following are low-glycemic-index dried fruits that can be kept for weeks or even months: dried apricots, cranberries, apple slices, mango slices, prunes, and raisins. Dried dates and

Have a small amount of granulated sugar and brown sugar on hand. I suggest taking no more than 25 grams (a little less than 2 tablespoons) of added sugar per person per day, used only to enhance the flavor of a dish rather than as a main ingredient—desserts included. It is good to have a jar of honey around as a substitute; although it is still made of sugars, it is more complex than regular sugar. Its composition is roughly 40 percent fructose, 30 percent glucose, 7 percent maltose, 5 percent other carbohydrates, 2 percent sucrose, 1 percent micronutrients, and 15 percent water; sugar from sugar cane or beet—sucrose—is half glucose and half fructose. The liquid form of honey also makes it suitable for glazing.

Keep a repertoire of spices—most of them should ideally be whole, unless it's too much trouble to grind at home. The flavors from the spices start to evaporate once they're ground, so use a grinder shortly before cooking, or better yet, grind them in a mortar and pestle, which crushes the cells under pressure to release more flavors. Spices should be stored in airtight containers, such as small glass jars, and kept in a dark place, such as inside a cabinet.

Have a collection of core spices: black peppercorns, mustard seeds, coriander seeds, fennel seeds, paprika, and dried chilies. Then add the following to create a bouquet of flavors: allspice, cloves, nutmeg, green cardamom pods, cinnamon, cumin seeds, star anise, white peppercorns, fenugreek seeds, caraway seeds, celery seeds, ground turmeric, and ground sumac.

These culinary herbs are best used when fresh: thyme, bay leaf, rosemary, parsley, oregano, cilantro (coriander), basil, dill, tarragon, marjoram, and sage. When that is impractical, spread them out on a sheet in a room with low humidity and dry them whole (they should dry out in 1–2 days). Store the dried herbs in a cool, dark place. When cooking, crush or chop the herbs and use them right away.

Vegetables and Fruits

Ideally, buy in-season and recently harvested produce and use within one or two days for maximum freshness and preservation of nutrients. If you have access to a farmers' market, by all means use it, though most of us have to rely on weekly trips to a grocery store to get our vegetables and fruits, and some of those should be stored in the refrigerator.

The following vegetables and fruits are best kept at room temperature either because they have thick skin and will keep, or because refrigeration compromises their flavors: tomato, onion, squash, beet (beetroot), carrot, cabbage, potato, sweet potato, avocado, and most fruits other than berries. Because tomatoes bring color and savory flavor to a dish, I like to have several kinds, as each has its own

texture, flavor, and use in cooking: plum tomato, salad tomato (beefsteak tomato), cherry tomato, and heirloom tomato. Get a few apples of each of the following characters, too: sweet, sour, crunchy, softer, green, yellow, and red. Potatoes and sweet potatoes have a high glycemic index, so eat them only occasionally.

Canned Foods

While I am not a fan of canned foods, I do have some in storage to serve special purposes.

Canned tomatoes: Because tomatoes lose flavor if exposed to cold temperature, sometimes canned tomatoes offer more flavor than "fresh" tomatoes that have been refrigerated, especially out of season.

Canned white kidney beans (cannellini beans), black beans, or other beans: These are versatile ingredients when you occasionally have to make a bean dish in a hurry.

Canned tuna in olive oil (not in water or sauce): Oil preserves the flavor better than water. Tuna is a good marine protein that can be used in a salad when you don't have time to cook fish from scratch. Fresh or frozen fish, though, has more nutrients than canned fish.

pasture-raised chicken and grass-fed beef when you can; they have richer micronutrients and more complex flavors. Fresh fish and shellfish are best bought and consumed the same or the next day for maximum freshness and cleanest flavor. See pages 12 and 190 for how to choose the freshest shellfish, otherwise they should be frozen. Shellfish, such as clams, mussels, crabs, and lobsters, will keep longer in a refrigerator (a couple days) if stored in a deep tray covered by wet paper towels to provide moisture. Don't keep them in closed plastic bags or they will perish.

Freezer

Keep some frozen fruit and vegetables in your freezer. They can sometimes be fresher than "fresh" produce because they were frozen quickly after harvesting instead of sitting in a container truck or in the supermarket produce bins for too long.

Also use your freezer to keep precooked sauces and stocks. It takes some time to make them, so when you do, make a large batch and freeze in small portions to add flavor to a dish in minutes.

Refrigerated

Vegetables and Fruits
In general, leafy vegetables and vegetables that don't have a thick skin to protect from loss of moisture—such as cucumber, zucchini (courgette), and eggplant (aubergine)—need to be stored unwashed in a bag or in the crisper drawer in a refrigerator, so they don't wither from loss of water. Mushrooms, scallions (spring onions), and garlic should be stored at room temperature for a few days, or in the refrigerator for a longer period of time. Store them in a paper bag to prevent buildup of condensation, which causes them to spoil more quickly.

Because berries do not have tough skins for protection and can get invisible bruises on their way to our homes, they can go bad quickly if kept at room temperature. Don't wash them until ready to eat, since washing bruises them. Store in small boxes to avoid them being squeezed under pressure, which also creates bruising. Most other fruits can be stored at room temperature.

Proteins
Have a container of unsweetened nondairy milk, such as almond milk, cashew milk, or soy milk, to use with breakfast cereals or when you need some creaminess in a dish. Keep a small supply of yogurt, kefir, cheese, and butter in the refrigerator. They can be used for variety and to enhance flavor in dishes.

In North America, eggs are usually refrigerated because they have been washed by the producers (removing their naturally protective coating). In Europe and other countries, they are usually stored at room temperature. Have an ample supply of eggs, as they are a good source of protein and micronutrients.

Poultry and meat can be stored in the refrigerator for a couple days, or the freezer for longer storage. Buy

How to Add Flavors

What makes a dish "delicious"?

Deliciousness comes from a combination of three different kinds of sensual stimulation, each felt by specific receptors in our mouth and nose: taste, smell, and texture. Taste comes from stimulation of chemical receptors in the mouth. Smell comes from stimulation of chemical receptors in the nose. Texture comes from stimulation of tactile receptors in the mouth and the esophagus. When the three are put together to match to a person's individual preference, formed by previous experience and cultural influences, "deliciousness" is born. Most people like sweetness, fattiness, and umami because they come from sugar, fat, and protein, each an essential nutrient for life. Keep these three senses in mind when you try to compose and execute a dish.

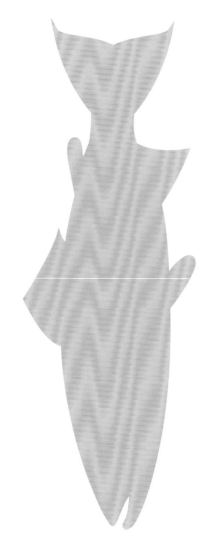

There are five basic tastes: salty, sweet, sour, bitter, and umami (savory). The first four are easy to understand and create. Umami is a bit more complex. Our tongue has five kinds of taste receptors, one for each of the above tastes. Therefore, these are the five fundamental tastes we can perceive, and all other taste sensations come from a combination of these. By making a collection of building blocks of intense flavors, we can assemble a dish with minimal effort, combining some simple cooking with one or two of these base blocks.

Saltiness

Saltiness is the foundation of taste in a dish. Sodium chloride—table salt—is the main electrolyte in the body, essential to life. In nature, salt is hard to get and precious, so our body developed this taste that helps us find salt and encourages us to eat more whenever we can. The problem with modern human life is that salt is too abundant and we end up eating more than we need—causing high blood pressure and fluid retention.

Saltiness usually comes from added salt, although some foods already contain sodium in their natural form, such as some seafood. Not all salts on the market are the same. Use sea salt when you can. Depending on where it is harvested, the impurities in sea salt, such as other electrolytes and microalgae, give it a unique taste. Try experimenting with different manufacturers and brands for subtle differences, then find the ones you like to stock in your kitchen. You will also need both fine and coarse salt. Coarse salt can be in a cubic, flaky, or pyramid crystal form. When used late in the cooking process, its crystal structures add a layer of texture stimulation or "crunch," which is desirable in some dishes. Kosher salt is in flaky crystals and sea salt is in cubic or pyramid crystals. Refined salt, like the plain iodized table salt, is just sodium chloride and rather boring.

Salty foods usually taste better, but too much salt is bad for the cardiovascular system. Dietary guidelines recommend less than 2,300 mg of sodium a day, which is roughly 1 teaspoon of salt—or ¼–½ teaspoon per meal. As you can see, we can easily exceed that amount if we are not mindful of it when cooking. One trick to reduce salt intake is to add a little bit of both sweet and sour taste when seasoning food. This enhances the sensation of saltiness, so you can use less salt to create the same flavor.

Sweetness

Sweetness comes from various forms of sugar. The most common forms are sucrose (when a chemical bond joins glucose with fructose), glucose, and fructose. Almost all food items contain some sugar. Most fruits have about 10 percent of their weight as a combination of sucrose, glucose, and fructose. Grapes and mango have about 15 percent, the highest of all fruits. Raspberries and strawberries have less, about 5 percent. The number is also around 5 percent for sweet vegetables such as carrots, sweet onions, or sweet peppers. Red beets (beetroot) have 7 percent, the highest among vegetables. Carbohydrates, once digested, turn into sugar (page 9). Simple carbohydrates ("white carbs," such as white bread, white rice, white potato) turn into sugar faster, thus can be problematic when you ingest a lot in a short period of time.

Most people like the sweet taste. However, excessive intake of sugar has been linked to many ailments. One doesn't need to totally avoid sugar for a healthy diet— this would be impossible and unnecessary. What we want to avoid is too much added sugar, which can cause hyperglycemic and insulin spikes, which are detrimental to health. "Added sugar" refers to sugars that are not naturally found in the ingredients themselves. So how much is "too much"? I usually use "less than 10 grams of added sugar per meal" as a yardstick, which is slightly less than 1 tablespoon. Total intake of added sugar should ideally be less than 25 grams a day. When making desserts, be mindful of how much sugar is allocated to each serving. If the dessert is very sweet, enjoy a spoonful but not the whole piece.

In cooking, added sugar usually comes in the form of sucrose crystals extracted from sugar beet or sugar cane. White sugar is almost pure sucrose, whereas brown sugar contains impurities from the original materials, which tend to give it a more complex flavor. Some dishes call for the use of white sugar, some brown sugar, others honey or syrup, such as maple syrup.

Certain cooking methods can convert sugar into flavorful substances that add to the tastiness and depth in a dish. For example, when heated to about 320°F (160°C), sugar, be it naturally occurring in the food ingredient or added during cooking, becomes caramelized, which gives the food a unique flavor and color. This is what happens when you caramelize onions, which contain some naturally occurring sugar. When heated to between 285°F (140°C) and 330°F (165°C), such as when browning meat, the sugar and protein in the food react to create the Maillard reaction. This reaction generates new substances that give the food complex flavors and increase its savoriness.

Sourness

Sourness comes from acidic substances. Common items used in cooking to create sourness are various fruits, such as lemon, lime, orange, apple, tomato, and tamarind; or fermented foods, such as vinegar, yogurt, pickled vegetables, and wine.

Acidity will make vegetables crunchier. Adding some vinegar when sautéing napa cabbage (Chinese leaf) or stir-frying bean sprouts, for example, gives them a firm rather than soft texture in the mouth. When marinating fish or meat with vinegar, lemon juice, or dry wine, the acidity facilitates the breakdown of protein to generate flavorful peptides, amino acids, and nucleotides, which tenderize proteins and add umami to the dish.

Vinegar is a versatile ingredient for adding acidity. It is made from the fermentation of grains, grapes, or apple cider. Vinegars tend to carry some flavors from the base food items used in fermentation. These distinct flavors can be used to give a dish character. Try rice vinegar, balsamic vinegar, red wine vinegar, and apple cider vinegar to appreciate these different flavors. Distilled white vinegar has a pure and clean taste, and is used when additional flavor is undesirable because it may mask or overwhelm a subtle dish.

Bitterness

While few people like the taste of bitterness in their food, in cooking this can be used to balance a dish. One can find bitterness in coffee, cocoa, many cruciferous vegetables (e.g., Brussels sprouts, arugula [rocket], watercress, radish), bitter melon (bitter gourd), hops, or charred foods.

For very sweet dishes, such as a dessert, a hint of bitterness from a little coffee or cocoa provides a refreshing balance. By the same token, if something is too bitter, add some sweetness. Throwing a few pieces of fruits such as orange or apple into an arugula salad can make it more interesting. Balance and complexity give a dish character and sophistication.

Umami

Umami refers to the savory taste that makes a dish "meaty," "rich," appetizing, and gives it depth. It tends to give a pleasant and satisfying aftertaste. Because the body needs amino acids and nucleotides (which are associated with the umami taste) to build cells, the ability to taste them helps us in seeking out foods rich in these nutrients.

One can create an umami-like taste by adding industrially made chemical products such as MSG (monosodium glutamate), but we can create umami naturally through fermentation or cooking methods. Cheeses, soy sauce, fish sauce, pickled vegetables, and cured meats are examples of fermented foods strong in umami. Sautéed mushrooms, homemade tomato sauce, anchovy paste, chicken stock, and vegetable stock are rich in umami generated by cooking methods.

Umami can also make a dish healthier. Many people feel saltiness makes a dish taste good, but too much salt is bad for the cardiovascular system, so adding a bit of umami to the dish means you will add less salt to achieve the same salty tastiness. Umami also creates satiety and reduces overeating. It makes a dish more appetizing, but you end up eating less to feel satisfied—the best of both worlds.

Other Tastes

Other tastes in foods are technically not "tastes" as they are not sensed by taste receptors in our mouth. They include spiciness (as in hot chilies, ginger, and garlic), astringency (as in tea and wine), coolness (as in mint), and numbness (as in Sichuan peppercorns).

The physical texture of the food is also important as an aspect of taste. How does the food feel in our mouth? Hard, soft, crunchy, mushy, dry, moist, grainy, smooth, heavy, fluffy, crisp, or sticky? Along with the five basic tastes, textures give us tools to create a large variety of interesting dishes.

Volatile Substances

Instead of just a handful of tastes, there are thousands of flavors in our foods. Flavors are perceived by the nose, or more precisely, the olfactory receptors located at the top part of the inside of our nose. Recall how uninteresting a food tastes and how much you miss in the eating experience when you have a stuffy nose. The combination of thousands of flavors and a handful of tastes gives us the endless possibilities of culinary enjoyment.

Flavors come from volatile organic compounds in the food. Warming or cooking food encourages these flavor molecules to come out into the air. So does chewing— chew thoroughly and exhale afterwards. This will bring the flavor up through the nose for us to smell it. This is part of the "mindful eating" discussed on page 13.

Many flavors are lipophilic, meaning they dissolve in fat or alcohol. Adding a bit of oil or wine while cooking helps bring the flavors out of the food ingredients. The same occurs when we marinate food with oil, alcohol, and spices.

Spices and herbs are concentrated flavor bombs. Use intact spices and fresh herbs whenever you can, and keep in mind that when a spice or herb is broken up, it starts to lose flavor. Grow some herbs at home if you can, so fresh herbs are readily available. If that is not feasible, buy fresh herbs and dry them intact. Keep the dried herbs in a cool, dark, and dry place to preserve the flavors in them.

When making a quick dish, such as a sautéed or stir-fried dish, crush or grind fresh spices with a mortar and pestle to break up the cells and release the volatile oils. You will see that the flavors are so much more intense and complex than those from bottled herbs and spices. When slow cooking, such as making stocks, soups,

or stews, use the whole spice or herb to let the flavor come out slowly over the entire cooking process. Use a spice sachet or bundle the herbs into a bouquet garni to make it easy to remove the whole herbs and spices.

Shortcuts to Flavor

Ideally, we want to make every dish from scratch, where everything is the freshest, and the best flavors are preserved. But not all of us have that time, at least not all the time. Here are some shortcuts:

1. Include a flavor-enhancing component in a dish. Now that we know the science of flavors, we can use that knowledge to make a flavor-packed dish in little time. Tomatoes, mushrooms, cheese, sauces, and stocks are our allies here.

2. Premake flavor-enhancing components and store them in small portions in the refrigerator or freezer. You can make a collection of core sauces and stocks, and when making a dish in a hurry, simply add the sauce or stock to make a plain dish sparkle.

3. Use overnight slow-cooking methods. Slow cooking is a healthy cooking method, which brings out more flavors from the foods, breaks down tough proteins and fibers, and makes the nutrients easy to digest and absorb. With a slow cooker you can just put the ingredients in the insert, mix them (and sometimes not), and hit the "on" button. The dish will be ready in a few hours. I also find slow cooking to be an underused function of the oven. You can put all the ingredients in a covered pot and put it in an oven set to 175°–225°F (80°–110°C) before you go to bed. The next morning you will have a perfectly slow-cooked, melt-in-your-mouth dish. It is almost like a higher temperature sous vide, without having to deal with the equipment and plastic bags. Throughout this book there are recipes for slow-cooked dishes.

4. Synchronize the cooking of different dishes to reduce time. When cooking multiple dishes for a meal, look at the recipes and plan accordingly. Some recipes call for a long hands-off cook time, such as in a stew or bake. Start this one first and use the hands-off time to cook others. By interlacing cook times this way, you can shorten the total time spent in the kitchen and have all the dishes ready to serve at about the same time.

Dos & Don'ts

Focus on the overall intake of foods, rather than occasional intakes. The effect of nutrients on your health is cumulative and long term. An occasional healthy food won't do you much good if your day-to-day regular diet is not healthy. By the same token, an occasional unhealthy food won't do you much harm either. The anxiety and guilt associated with not being able to always stick to a "perfect diet" can be more harmful.

Eat more "real" foods made at home. Reduce the number of premade foods or those that come in a box or can. Avoid highly processed food ingredients and those with many additives.

Eat a plant-based diet. It doesn't have to be totally vegetarian or vegan, but the majority of ingredients should come from plants—about 80 percent of your overall intake.

The key words are "complexity" and "balance." A meal consisting of a variety of different kinds of foods is better than just a few so-called "superfoods," because the body needs thousands of nutrients, which no single superfood can provide.

Aim for balanced portions and proportions of vegetables, proteins, and carbohydrates. About half the plate (two-quarters) should be vegetables and/or fruits, one-quarter protein, and one-quarter carbohydrates. Add some healthy plant-based oil and plenty of liquid. Each quarter-size serving on the plate should be no more than the size of your fist.

Pick foods by their colors. The vegetable part of your plate should be a rainbow (green, red, yellow, purple, etc.); the protein part light in color (nuts, beans, egg white, fish, shellfish); the carbohydrate part dark in color (whole wheat, brown rice, other whole grains).

Use fresh ingredients whenever you can. Many nutrients are not very stable once harvested. When shopping, pick up the produce and smell it. If it has lost its original scent, it is not very fresh. Sometimes frozen vegetables are useful during off-season because they tend to be preserved shortly after harvesting.

Eat more cruciferous vegetables. These vegetables, which include broccoli, Brussels sprouts, cabbage, cauliflower, collard greens, and kale, are particularly healthy. Eat fewer starchy vegetables like potatoes.

9

Eat two to four servings daily of low-sugar fruits (berries, apples, apricots, citrus, kiwis). Limit—but no need to totally avoid—high-glycemic fruits such as grapes, mango, and watermelon.

10

Limit meat in general, especially red meat. If you love meat, an occasional meat dish is fine and won't cause harm in the bigger scheme of things. Definitely minimize processed meat.

11

Replace animal fats with plant-based oils. Limit the use of butter in your cooking. Replace it as often as possible with oils, such as olive oil or canola (rapeseed) oil.

12

Limit "added sugar" intake. Consume less than 25 grams per day or 10 grams per meal. Read labels to find out how much added sugar is in a food. Small amounts—1 teaspoon of sugar (around 2–3 grams) in coffee, a small piece of dark chocolate—are fine.

13

Drink room-temperature water or warm fluids. Soup and noncaffeinated teas are good choices. Aim for six to eight 8-ounce (250 ml) glasses daily. Spread the fluid intake throughout the day.

14

Limit alcohol and caffeine intake. Coffee and tea in moderation are fine if these do not affect your sleep cycles. And a glass of wine with dinner a couple times a week is fine, however too much hard liquor can affect the liver.

15

Use gentle cooking methods with low temperatures: boiling, steaming, baking, and sautéing. Limit grilling proteins in the presence of fat, which brings the food into direct contact with flame and smoke and can produce harmful compounds. An occasional quick broil is fine. Minimize deep-fried foods, barbecued, and smoked foods.

16

Try to eat at the same times every day and walk for five minutes after meals. This promotes transition of the food through the digestive tract. Eat a large breakfast and lunch, then a smaller early dinner. Do not eat during the three hours before bedtime.

17

Eat all calories in a ten- to twelve-hour window. For example, breakfast at 8 a.m., dinner by 7 p.m., and no snacks after dinner.

18

Practice mindful eating. Slow down and savor the look, smell, taste, and texture of the food. Chew at least ten times before swallowing.

Healthy Living Beyond the Plate

Nutrition is an important part of the foundation for good health. But it is not the whole story. Most diseases are the result of three factors combined: the disease-causing agent, the environment, and the host. For example, the seriousness of a viral infection depends on how aggressive the virus is, the circumstance in which the virus came into contact with the host, and how strong the host's constitution is (the immune system, the metabolic landscape, etc.).

Therefore, if we are in good health, we are less likely to get sick when exposed to the same thing that otherwise causes disease and, if we do get sick, more likely to have a mild case and recover faster. Nutrients alone cannot keep us in top shape. We need more. There are several elements we can tend to for optimal wellness, and I will talk a little more about some core principles of health—nutrition, exercise, stress management, sleep and circadian rhythm, social environment, finding "joy" in life, digestive health, and complementary therapies—in the following pages.

Why do we need to take care of these elements? Think of the body as a plant. There is an intrinsic ability to adapt, thrive, and heal in every life, be it a plant or a human. Most of the time, simply giving it what it needs is enough. A plant needs the right amount of water and nutrients from the soil; we need a proper mix of nutrients from our diet. A plant needs to see the right amount of sunlight—scalded when too much and withering when too little; we need the right amount of physical exercise—too much or too little can both do harm. A plant needs to have the ability itself, or be able to get extra help, to fend off pests; we need to have the ability or the help to manage stress. A plant needs to experience the proper day/night temperature cycles and seasonal changes; we need a regular circadian rhythm for our daily activities and high-quality sleep. A plant likes the right kind of soil in terms of acidity and drainage; we need to live in a healthy physical environment and supportive social environment. A plant enjoys the tender loving care of a gardener; we need to find joy, love, and meaning in our life. In addition, a plant benefits from the symbiotic relationship it has with little friends like bees, butterflies, and earthworms; we have trillions of microbes in our body to help it stay healthy. Occasionally a plant needs some pruning to

rejuvenate its growth; we can use some holistic therapies to help us maintain wellbeing.

And these elements need to be tended to regularly. We cannot abuse our body with smoking and drinking most of the time, then do a week-long "detox." We cannot eat junk food most days, then have a healthy meal from time to time. We cannot stay sedentary in front of a computer all day during the week, then run a 5K on the weekend. Human physiology just doesn't work that way. It needs regular, long-term exposure to things that strengthen us, and a general avoidance of things that undermine us. Our bodies need daily cultivation. This awareness is important.

Maintaining health and wellness is a holistic process. It is like a barrel with many planks. If one plank is short, the barrel will leak water, no matter how long or strong the other planks are. To achieve optimal health, we need to pay attention to all those aspects—beyond what is on our plate.

⇻ Nutrition

Good nutrition does not rely on a few "superfoods."
It focuses on a consistent healthy eating habit,
practiced over years. Eat a plant-based diet, select
high-quality fresh ingredients, maintain the proper
ratio of macronutrients, focus on the complexity and
balance of the numerous micronutrients, use healthy
cooking methods, and practice mindful eating.
If you adhere to these few principles, your nutrition
will be well taken care of. An occasional divergence
is nothing to feel anxious or guilty about. In short,
eat "less and more." Less quantity, more quality.

↠ Physical Exercise

Physical exercise not only keeps our heart and lungs strong and builds muscle, it can also trigger a cellular process—autophagy—that literally "cleans" the body's cells and keeps them healthy. Like cleaning our home, it should be done often— ideally daily! I call exercise "the fourth meal of the day," which means that it should become a natural part of your regular rhythm. I like walking because it can be done anytime, anywhere, and it is a fundamental physical ability that we need to maintain as we get older. Swimming is also excellent as it combines aerobic and resistance exercise. Exercising at moderate intensity (heart rate up a bit and sweating a bit) for thirty minutes once or twice a day will ensure you feel the health benefits while still being very sustainable.

↠ Stress Management

Stressors are inevitable in life, but our reaction to them can be modified to reduce the toll of stress on our health. One self-care stress management approach I recommend is a mind-body practice such as mindfulness meditation—focusing our awareness on the present moment without judgment. It should not be seen as a short-term escape from problems. Think of it as a life skill, like knowing how to swim. And just like swimming, it takes regular practice. Incorporate it into the routine things you do every day. Start small with mindful eating (page 13) and home cooking, where you're fully immersed in the culinary processes. Then perform other daily activities with that same mindset. Once learned and practiced regularly, it will allow you to handle stress and retain a sense of calm.

→ Sleep and Rhythms

Sleep should be high on the priority list when we time-manage our days. If you have deep, refreshing sleep, you may sleep fewer hours and still feel energized, thus freeing up valuable time. It helps to go to bed at the same time every day and practice a pre-sleep routine to quiet the mind: Listen to relaxing music, take a hot shower or bath, do gentle yoga stretches and mindfulness meditation, and cut out all screen time at least thirty minutes before bedtime. If you set an alarm clock at all, it should not be for the morning, it should be for the evening—to remind you that it is time to go to bed. In addition to sleeping at set hours, develop a daily rhythm for other activities as well. Get up at the same time every day. Eat each meal at the same time. Exercise at the same time. The body likes regularity.

⇒ Social Environment

Humans are social animals, and social interactions are important to our physical and mental health– eating together, working together, having fun together, and exchanging ideas together. Our relationships with our family, friends, co-workers, and other people in our communities create this social environment. When it is supportive, we are happier, healthier, more productive, and we live longer. Take a pulse of your specific social environment, nurture strong, healthy relationships, and identify areas for improvement. In addition, the physical environment we live in also affects our health. If we live in a dirty, cluttered, and disorganized physical space, neither our body nor our mind will feel well. One simple trick is to declutter your home from time to time. You will find many items that are not needed or important to you, and you will feel surprisingly good afterward.

⇉ Love and the Meaning of Life

Make sure you take "Vitamin L" every day—love, light, and laughter! In addition to your physical and emotional wellbeing, you also need to take care of your spiritual wellbeing. Allocate a little time for self-care every day, dedicated to doing something you love, that brings you peace and joy and gives meaning, be it reading a book, listening to music, or working on a passion. Pause from time to time to check: Did I have fun today? Did I laugh today? Did I express kindness to someone today? Just before you sleep, think about all those things you are grateful for today; and when you wake, focus for a moment on the one thing that is most meaningful for you to achieve during the coming day. You could expand this to encompass the week, month, and year ahead, allowing you to truly focus your mind and energy on the important things in your life.

→ Digestive Health

Trillions of microbes live naturally in our gut. This community of hundreds of species of microbes, called microbiota, are shaped by our diet and cooking methods. They digest foods for us, generate certain unique nutrients, interact with the immune system, and produce substances that influence our metabolism, immunity, and even our behaviors. For example, a diet rich in fiber and fish encourages the growth of microbes that help reduce inflammation, diabetes, and obesity, when compared to a diet rich in meat. When we have a healthy microbiota, one that is diverse and includes all the beneficial microbes, these microscopic allies help us maintain health. The healthy eating principles discussed in this book promote a microbiota that has been associated with better health. Prebiotics (fiber) and probiotics (fermented food eaten uncooked) are particularly relevant for the microbiota. Make sure they are part of your diet.

⇸ Complementary Therapy

Not every remedy comes in the form of a pill or procedure targeting a specific ailment. Some therapies from ancient medical systems, such as acupuncture, massage, and yoga, tend to take a holistic approach and address the body as an interconnected whole. Their therapeutic effects have been studied recently and validated for certain clinical problems. These include aches and pains, tension, anxiety, insomnia, nausea, and digestive problems, which do not respond to conventional treatments or when conventional treatments have hard-to-tolerate side effects. They are increasingly used to complement medical or surgical treatments to improve quality of life and wellbeing. Consider them as part of a comprehensive wellness plan.

Breakfast

Whole-Wheat Pancakes

Pancakes made with white flour and sugar, topped with syrup, tend to be high in refined carbohydrates and raise the glucose level in the blood. White flour has the outer bran layer and the germ of the wheat berries removed, losing fiber, B vitamins, and minerals. I use whole-wheat flour to reduce the glycemic index of this dish and preserve more of the micronutrients. I replace milk with kefir or yogurt, which is more flavorful and easier to digest. I also use less syrup. The result has fewer than 10 grams of added sugar per serving.

Preparation time: 10 minutes
Cooking time: 15 minutes
Serves 4

* 1 cup (120 g) whole-wheat flour
* 2 teaspoons sugar
* 1 teaspoon baking powder
* ½ teaspoon baking soda (bicarbonate of soda)
* ¼ teaspoon kosher (flaked) salt
* 1 cup (280 g) plain kefir or European-style yogurt (i.e., runny yogurt)
* 1 egg, beaten
* 1 tablespoon canola (rapeseed) oil
* 1 cup (120–150 g) fresh berries, such as blueberries, raspberries, blackberries, or sliced strawberries
* 1 banana, thinly sliced
* 2 tablespoons pure maple syrup

1. In a large bowl, whisk together the flour, sugar, baking powder, baking soda (bicarbonate of soda), and salt and mix to combine evenly.

2. Add the kefir and egg. Mix until it becomes a thick but still pourable batter. (A few clumps in the batter is okay.) Add a little lukewarm water, if needed, to achieve this consistency. Let the batter rest for about 5 minutes.

3. Heat a large seasoned cast-iron skillet over medium heat. Brush with half of the canola (rapeseed) oil. Stir the batter and pour half into the skillet. Spread to about ¼ inch (6 mm) thick by tilting and swirling the skillet. Reduce the heat to medium-low. You will see little bubbles start to appear on the surface. Cook until the bubbling has stopped, the surface becomes matte, and the bottom is lightly golden, 3–5 minutes. Flip and cook the other side until golden, 2–3 minutes. Repeat to make a second pancake.

4. Divide the pancakes among four plates: Quarter each pancake and stack two quarters on each plate. Top with the berries, banana slices, and maple syrup.

> → *Pairs with* ←
> A breakfast protein (an egg-, tofu-, or yogurt-based dish), plus 2 servings of fresh fruit or a smoothie, for a complete breakfast.

Yogurt Cup with Mixed Berries and Nuts

Yogurt is a good source of protein for breakfast or as a snack. Although an animal protein, the fermentation process breaks it down and makes it easy to digest. The process also produces an abundance of probiotics, which enhance gut health and immunity. The quality of yogurt is determined by the quality of the milk used to make it: Ideally, find one made from organic milk that is low-fat or fat-free, to reduce the intake of milk fat if you eat yogurt often. Drained yogurt (e.g., Greek-style yogurt or Icelandic skyr) is thicker, with a higher protein content, making it more filling than regular yogurt. Yogurt with live probiotics ("active cultures") is usually labeled as such. Check the label to find the amount of sugar added—it should contain no more than 10 grams of sugar per serving, or at most 15 grams.

Preparation time: ⑤ minutes
Serves ④

* 2½ cups (700 g) plain low-fat yogurt (ideally organic with active cultures)
* 1 cup (130 g) raspberries, fresh or thawed frozen
* 1 cup (150 g) blueberries, fresh or thawed frozen
* 1 cup (150 g) unsalted roasted or raw whole nuts or seeds, such as walnuts, pecans, sunflower seeds, pumpkin seeds, hazelnuts, macadamia nuts, cashew nuts, pistachio nuts, or Brazil nuts (or any combination)

1. Divide the yogurt equally among four medium bowls.

2. Top each with ¼ cup raspberries, ¼ cup blueberries, and ¼ cup nuts and seeds.

> → *Pairs with* ←
> Any hot cereal or
> toast dish, plus ②
> servings of fresh fruit
> or a smoothie, for a
> complete breakfast.

Almond Milk
Vegan Protein Shake

Nut milk is a healthy substitute for cow's milk. Whey protein is often used in protein shakes for those who eat dairy—it is a "complete protein" (containing all nine essential amino acids in adequate amounts) and easy to digest. But to make this protein shake vegan, I use a combination of pea protein and rice protein. Both contain all the essential amino acids, but pea protein is a little low in the amino acid methionine, and rice protein is low in the amino acid lysine. When combined, however, they complement and complete each other. The fat in coconut oil can be more readily absorbed by the body than other fats, and is a good source of energy. Chia seeds swell up in the presence of water, which, along with the banana and coconut oil, gives the shake a thick and creamy consistency. Both chia seeds and flaxseeds are high in omega-3 fatty acids, a nutrient helpful in reducing inflammation.

Preparation time: ①⓪ minutes
Serves ④

* 3 cups (25 fl oz/750 ml) unsweetened almond milk or cashew milk
* 3 oz (80 g) plain unsweetened pea protein powder
* 3 oz (80 g) rice protein powder
* 1 banana, broken into pieces
* 1 tablespoon unsweetened cocoa powder
* 1 tablespoon coconut oil
* 1 tablespoon chia seeds
* 1 tablespoon flaxseeds (optional)
* Garnish: mint leaves, pomegranate seeds, coconut flakes, sliced almonds, or cacao nibs

1. In a large blender (see *Note*), combine the almond milk, 3 cups (25 fl oz/750 ml) room-temperature water, both protein powders, banana, cocoa powder, coconut oil, chia seeds, and flaxseeds (if using).

2. Blend at high speed until very smooth.

3. Divide between four glasses. Add your choice of garnish and serve.

Note: Depending on the size and power of your blender, you may have to do this in two or more batches.

> → *Pairs with* ←
> Any hot cereal or toast dish, plus ② servings of fresh fruit, for a complete breakfast.

Millet Porridge

Millet is an ancient grain. The little seeds are rich in fiber and low in glycemic index, making millet a complex carbohydrate that doesn't create a sugar spike. It is very balanced in B vitamins, while other grains may be rich in one B vitamin but not another. This recipe contains about half of all the vitamin B2, B3, B5, B6, and B9 a person needs in a day. If you get bored with oatmeal for breakfast, try using millet cooked in a similar way.

Preparation time: ⑤ minutes
Cooking time: ①⑤ minutes
Serves: ④

* 1 cup (200 g) millet
* Pinch of baking soda (bicarbonate of soda) or baking powder (optional)
* 2 apples, sliced thinly
* ½ cup (85 g) raisins

1. Place the millet in a fine-mesh sieve and rinse well.

2. In a small saucepan, combine the millet with 4–6 cups (32–48 fl oz/950 ml–1.4 liters) water (use the smaller amount of water for a thicker porridge) and the baking soda (bicarbonate of soda), if using (see *Note*).

3. Bring to a boil over high heat. Reduce the heat to medium-low and simmer vigorously, uncovered. (The heat should be high enough for the millet to tumble but not so high that the liquid spills over. Reduce the heat if it starts to foam and spill over.) Simmer until your desired consistency, 10–15 minutes if you prefer a coarse mouthfeel and up to 15–20 minutes if you prefer it creamier.

4. Transfer to four serving bowls and top with the apple slices and raisins.

Note: The baking soda or baking powder adds a bit of alkalinity, which speeds up the degradation of starch and makes the cereal thicken more quickly, releasing substances that give the dish a different fragrance profile.

> → *Pairs with* ←
> A breakfast protein (an egg- or tofu-based dish), plus ② servings of fresh fruit, for a complete breakfast.

Granola with Mixed Seeds and Grains

Granola is not hard to make at home. It is much better than store-bought granola because you can control what goes into it and how much sugar is used. This recipe leaves much room for improvisation. You can use any nuts and seeds you like, in any ratio, so you can change the composition every week for variety. The recipe can be scaled up easily and you can store leftovers in the freezer for a few weeks—ready to eat at a moment's notice. This breakfast is high in healthy protein, fat, and fiber, and low in carbohydrates. It only has about 10 grams of added sugar per serving—lower than most commercial granola products.

Preparation time: 10 minutes
Cooking time: 10 minutes
Serves: 4

* 2 cups (300 g) mixed raw nuts and seeds, such as almonds, pumpkin seeds, sunflower seeds, walnuts, hazelnuts, flaxseeds, or peanuts
* 2 cups (180 g) rolled oats
* 4 tablespoons unsweetened almond butter, sunflower seed butter, or peanut butter (see *Note 1*)
* 2 tablespoons honey
* 2 tablespoons jarred date preserves or date bits (see *Note 2*)
* Pinch of fine sea salt

1. Preheat the oven to 350°F (180°C/Gas Mark 4).

2. Spread the nuts/seeds and oats on a sheet pan and bake until toasted, about 10 minutes. Let cool.

3. Transfer the mixture to a blender or food processor and pulse to break into small pieces (see *Note 3*). Transfer to a large bowl and stir in the nut/seed butter, honey, date preserves, and salt. Toss with a spoon to combine, pressing down with the spoon to make small clumps.

4. The granola can be eaten right away or pressed into silicone ice cube trays and frozen. When ready to eat, just leave them to thaw at room temperature.

Note 1: If the nut or seed butter is too firm for easy mixing, soften it first by microwaving for 10–15 seconds.

Note 2: An alternative to date preserves is to buy pitted dried dates or figs and soak them in water for 1–2 hours to rehydrate. Process to small pieces in a blender or coffee grinder.

Note 3: This granola is quite soft, which I like. If you like a more traditional crunchy granola, add 2 tablespoons water during mixing, which dissolves the starch in the oats and bonds the mixture. Spread back on the sheet pan and toast for another 10–15 minutes at 325°F (160°C/Gas Mark 3) to crisp it up. Cool and store at room temperature for a few days.

→ *Pairs with* ←
A smoothie and a bowl of berries for a complete breakfast.

Oatmeal with Fruit and Nuts

Oats are a gluten-free breakfast cereal full of healthy fiber. Here, I pair them with fruit for the vegetables-and-fruits component, and nuts for the protein component, to make a balanced dish. If you want the oatmeal firmer, wait until the water starts boiling before adding the oats; the outer layer quickly forms a hard-to-penetrate gel and will keep the inside from overcooking. If you use steel-cut (Scotch) oats, increase the cooking time by 10–15 minutes; oat groats may need 20–30 minutes or more. If you like it a bit thicker, reduce the water by about 1 cup (8 fl oz/250 ml). For a healthier oatmeal, omit the milk.

Preparation time: ⑤ minutes
Cooking time: ①⓪ minutes
Serves: ④

* 2 cups (180 g) rolled oats
* 2 cups (16 fl oz/475 ml) unsweetened nut milk (optional), warmed
* 2 cups (240–300 g) fresh fruit or 1 cup (160 g) dried fruit (see *Note*)
* 2 cups (300 g) nuts and/or seeds (see *Note*), raw or toasted
* Pinch of ground spices (optional), such as cinnamon or nutmeg

1. In a medium saucepan, combine the oats and 6 cups (48 fl oz /1.4 liters) cold water if not using nut milk, or 4 cups (32 fl oz / 950 ml) if adding nut milk later.

2. Bring to a boil over medium-high heat and simmer uncovered until thickened, 2–3 minutes, stirring occasionally to prevent the oats from sticking to the bottom of the pot. Remove from the heat. If using nut milk, stir it in now.

3. Pour the cooked oatmeal into four bowls. Top with the fruit and nuts of your choice. Sprinkle with spices, if desired.

Note: For fruits, use fresh fruits such as blueberries or strawberries and dried fruits such as apricots and cranberries. For nuts and seeds, use walnuts, pecans, almonds, or sunflower seeds. Mix up your combinations of fruits and nuts to add variety. For example, use blueberries, dried cranberries, and pecans one day, and dried apricots, walnuts, and sunflower seeds another.

> → *Pairs with* ←
> A breakfast protein (an egg- or tofu-based dish), plus a serving of fresh fruit, for a complete breakfast, or eat as a stand-alone light breakfast.

Chia Seed Pudding

Chia seeds have all of the good nutrients: One-third of their weight is fiber, one-third plant oil, one-sixth plant protein, and the rest useful minerals such as calcium, magnesium, potassium, and phosphorus. What's more, 60 percent of the oil is omega-3, the healthier type of fatty acid, on a par with flaxseeds—that's more omega-3 than the same weight of salmon; just 2 tablespoons will give you 20 percent of the calcium you need each day. The seeds don't have much of a taste on their own, so use your imagination to add flavorful ingredients to create variety. This recipe only takes a few minutes of hands-on time to make—layer it up in glass jars or cups and you'll have a pretty and easy breakfast for the entire week.

Preparation time: ①⑤ minutes,
plus overnight soaking
Serves: ④
For vegan, use sweetened nut milk;
for nut-free, use honey and oat milk

* 1 tablespoon honey or a sweetened
  nut milk
* 4¼ cups (34 fl oz/1 liter)
  unsweetened almond milk, cashew
  milk, coconut milk, or oat milk
* ½–¾ cup (80–120 g) chia seeds,
  depending on preferred thickness
* 4 oz (120 g) natural flavoring
  (see *Note*)
* 1 cup (120–150 g) berries, one variety
  or mixed

1. In a large glass jar or bowl, whisk the honey into your chosen milk.

2. Mix in the chia seeds to coat them evenly in the liquid. Let sit until the seeds swell up a bit, about 10 minutes.

3. Stir again to redistribute the seeds and make sure none are clumping. Cover and refrigerate overnight until thickened.

4. Line the bases of four small glass jars or cups with the flavoring. Divide the chia mixture between the jars. Top with the berries.

Note: For the flavoring, use something colorful you already have in your refrigerator, such as leftover boiled sweet potato or green pea purée, freshly sliced strawberries, or diced pineapple or cantaloupe melon.

> → *Pairs with* ←
> A vegetable smoothie for
> a light breakfast. It can
> also serve as a dessert for
> lunch or dinner.

Kasha

Buckwheat groats can be used like steel-cut (Scotch) oats to make hot breakfast cereal. The resulting porridge is called kasha, popular in Eastern European cultures. Hot cereal is preferable to cold cereal for breakfast as it doesn't chill and stress the digestive tract as much. Kasha is gluten-free, fiber-rich, and packed with magnesium, manganese, and niacin—1 cup (170 g) will provide half of your daily needs. Kasha is not as slippery as oatmeal and has a more defined texture—a good choice for those who like variation in their breakfast cereal. When cooked with less water as a grain, it can also serve as the carbohydrate element of any full meal, replacing quinoa or other grain berries. You can enjoy this dish plain, sweet, or savory—for savory, consider adding a tablespoonful of stock, soy sauce, or gluten-free tamari instead of the sweet option in the recipe.

Preparation time: ⑤ minutes
Cooking time: ②⓪ minutes
Serves ④

* 1½ cups (255 g) buckwheat groats
* 2 teaspoons ground cinnamon
* 1 cup (120–150 g) mixed berries and/or cherries

1. Rinse the groats with water to remove any loose debris (see *Note*).

2. In a small saucepan, combine the kasha and 3 cups (25 fl oz/750 ml) water. Bring to a boil over high heat, stirring occasionally to prevent the groats from sticking to the bottom of the pan. Reduce the heat to a simmer, cover, and cook to the desired firmness, 15–20 minutes.

3. Sprinkle over the cinnamon and serve with the fresh fruit.

Note: Rinsing off any debris will give the kasha a cleaner taste and better texture. Add cold water to a saucepan containing the groats and stir. The loose debris should float to the top. Pour off the water gently without disturbing the groats that have settled on the bottom. Repeat until no more debris is loosened and the water becomes totally clear.

> ⇢ *Pairs with* ⇠
> A breakfast protein (an egg- or yogurt-based dish or protein shake), plus ② servings of fresh fruit or a smoothie, for a complete breakfast. Pair with any salad or vegetable dish, plus a protein dish, for a complete lunch or dinner.

Green Smoothie

Smoothies can be ready in just a few minutes for a quick, healthy breakfast. They should contain some fat and protein to facilitate absorption of vitamins and give the smoothie a creamy consistency—it is okay to use milk or yogurt occasionally, but plant oils and proteins, such as the avocado and nut butter used here, are preferable. This smoothie is rich in vitamins A, D, K, and E, and instead of adding sugar or syrup for sweetness, I opt for healthier honey.

Preparation time: 10 minutes
Serves 4

* 3 oz (80 g) spinach leaves (mature spinach if high fiber is desired, baby spinach if not)
* 3 oz (80 g) kale leaves (mature kale if high fiber is desired, baby kale if not)
* 8 kiwifruits, peeled and cut into chunks
* 2 apples with skin, sliced
* 1 Hass avocado, halved and pitted (destoned)
* 2 tablespoons honey
* 4 tablespoons unsweetened nut butter
* Red garnish, such as saffron threads, goji berries, pomegranate seeds, or dried cranberries

1. In a large blender (see *Note*), combine the spinach, kale, kiwifruits, apples, and 2–4 cups (16–32 fl oz/475–950 ml) water at room temperature (use less water for a thicker smoothie). Blend at high speed to break up the leaves.

2. Scoop in the avocado flesh and add the honey and nut butter. Blend again until very smooth.

3. Pour into glasses, garnish, and serve.

Note: Depending on the size and power of your blender, you may need to do this in two or more batches.

> ↠ *Pairs with* ↞
> A cereal or toast, a breakfast protein (an egg-, tofu-, or yogurt-based dish), plus a serving of fresh fruit, for a complete breakfast. Or drink on its own as a quick and light breakfast.

Red Smoothie

This smoothie is full of red pigments—red-colored antioxidants that help protect cells from environmental damage. Raspberries are particularly high in vitamin C, manganese, and fiber, and in this smoothie they provide one-third of what our body needs daily from those three nutrients.

Preparation time: 10 minutes
Cooking time: 15 minutes (if using raw beets)
Serves: 4
For vegan, choose an appropriate garnish

* 2 medium raw beets (beetroot) or 2 cooked beets
* 2 medium tomatoes, cut into small chunks
* 1 cup (130 g) raspberries
* 2 large bananas, broken into pieces
* 4 tablespoons unsweetened nut butter
* White garnish, such as coconut shreds, sliced almonds, pine nuts, or white chocolate flakes

1. If using raw beets (beetroot), place them in a small saucepan with water to cover. Bring to a boil and simmer until completely cooked through, about 15 minutes. Let cool, remove the skin, and cut into small chunks. If using cooked, cut them into chunks

2. In a large blender (see *Note*), combine the beets, tomatoes, raspberries, bananas, nut butter, and 2–4 cups (16–32 fl oz/475–950 ml) room-temperature water (use less water for a thicker smoothie). Blend on high until very smooth.

3. Pour into glasses, garnish, and serve.

Note: Depending on the size and power of your blender, you may need to do this in two or more batches.

> → *Pairs with* ←
> A cereal or toast, a breakfast protein (an egg-, tofu-, or yogurt-based dish), plus a serving of fresh fruit, for a complete breakfast. Or drink on its own as a quick and light breakfast.

Yellow Smoothie

Keep on the skin of the cucumbers and apples to provide fiber in this smoothie. Celery is also very high in fiber, and turmeric has anti-inflammatory properties, so this refreshing smoothie has a great detox effect. Blending turmeric with coconut oil or coconut butter makes it easier to absorb, enabling it to do its work in the body.

Preparation time: ①⓪ minutes
Serves: ④

* 2 medium Kirby cucumbers (or 6 Persian/mini cucumbers) with skin, cut into small chunks
* 4 stalks celery from a celery heart, cut into small chunks
* 2 yellow apples with skin, sliced
* 4 teaspoons ground turmeric or 1 tablespoon sliced fresh turmeric root
* 4 tablespoons coconut oil or coconut butter (the latter for more coconut flavor)
* Green garnish, such as mint leaves, dill leaves, microgreens, or chopped parsley

1. In a large blender (see *Note*), combine the cucumbers, celery, apples, turmeric, coconut oil, and 2–4 cups (16–32 fl oz/ 475–950 ml) room-temperature water (use less water for a thicker smoothie). Blend on high until very smooth.

2. Pour into glasses, garnish, and serve.

Note: Depending on the size and power of your blender, you may need to do this in two or more batches.

> ⇻ *Pairs with* ⇺
> A cereal or toast, a breakfast protein (an egg-, tofu-, or yogurt-based dish), plus a serving of fresh fruit, for a complete breakfast. Or drink on its own as a quick and light breakfast.

Avocado Toast with Toppings

Instead of spreading butter on toast, try olive oil, nut butter, or avocado for a flavorful yet plant-based option. Use slices of well-toasted multigrain or whole-wheat sourdough bread to form a firm foundation for the toppings. This is a very versatile breakfast dish, in which the toast and avocado serve as a blank canvas for you to paint a colorful picture. Use your imagination and experiment with various toppings.

Preparation time: ①⑤ minutes
Cooking time: ⑤ minutes
Serves: ④
For vegan/vegetarian, choose an appropriate topping option

* 4 large or 8 medium slices whole-grain or multigrain bread
* 2 medium Hass avocados (about 6 oz/175 g each), halved and pitted (destoned)
* Pinch of kosher (flaked) salt
* Dash of fresh lime juice
* 2 cloves garlic, peeled and whole (optional)

1. In a toaster (or a cast-iron skillet over medium heat), toast both sides of the bread until lightly golden brown and the surface is firm and crunchy, 2–5 minutes.

2. While the bread is being toasted, scoop the avocado flesh into a flat-bottomed bowl. (It's harder to break up the avocado in a round-bottomed bowl because it moves around too much.) Use a fork to mash the avocado to a mixture of paste and chunks—so not totally mashed. Mix in the salt and lime juice to bring the avocado alive.

3. If you like garlic bread, rub the garlic cloves on the toast, using the toasted surface as a garlic grater.

4. Spread the avocado on top of the toast, about ½ inch (1.25 cm) thick. Add your topping of choice.

Topping options

For a Mexican flavor: Finely chopped red onion, cilantro (coriander), red bell pepper, and a pinch of coarse sea salt.

For an Italian flavor: Chopped tomato, sweet basil, a dash of extra-virgin olive oil, and a pinch of kosher (flaked) salt.

For a Chinese flavor: Scrambled egg with mushrooms and chopped scallion (spring onion).

For a Southeast Asian flavor: Crushed peanuts, diced apple, chopped Thai basil, a dash of sriracha, and a dash of fish sauce (optional).

For a Middle Eastern flavor: Zhoug or harissa, chopped parsley, sesame seeds, pomegranate seeds, ground cumin, and toasted almonds or sunflower seeds.

> ⇝ *Pairs with* ⇜
> A breakfast protein (an egg- or yogurt-based dish or protein shake), plus ② servings of fresh fruit or a smoothie, for a complete breakfast. Pair with any salad or vegetable dish, plus a protein dish, for a complete lunch or dinner.

Nut-Butter Multigrain Toast with Poached Fruits

Toast is a staple breakfast food, but regular white bread toast with butter and jam is high in simple carbohydrates and saturated fat. I use multigrain to replace white bread, nut butter to replace cow's milk butter, and poached fruit to replace jam or jelly. The carbohydrates in white bread are mainly from white flour, but multigrain bread includes other grains and seeds, so it has more fiber, B vitamins, vitamin E, and minerals. Nut butter has more unsaturated fat than butter and is dairy-free. I like sunflower seed butter for its distinct taste, but use your favorite unsweetened nut butter. Finally, the quick-poached fruit I make here is sweetened by cooking in its own juices, so it doesn't have any added sugar as both jam and jelly do.

Preparation time: ⑤ minutes
Cooking time: ①⑤ minutes
Serves ④

* 4 medium apples, pears, peaches, or plums (or a combination), unpeeled and cut into slices ½ inch (1.25 cm) thick
* 4 slices multigrain or whole-wheat bread
* 4 tablespoons unsweetened nut or seed butter, such as sunflower seed butter, almond butter, or peanut butter

1. In a medium saucepan, combine the sliced fruit with enough water to just barely cover the fruit. Bring to a boil, then reduce the heat to a simmer. Cover and cook until the fruit is tender and translucent, 7–10 minutes, depending on the fruit you've chosen. Drain off any excess water.

2. Toast the bread to your desired doneness.

3. Spread the nut butter on the toast, top with the poached fruit slices, and serve.

> → *Pairs with* ←
> A breakfast protein (an egg- or yogurt-based dish or protein shake), plus ② servings of fresh fruit or a smoothie, for a complete breakfast. Pair with any salad or vegetable dish, plus a protein dish, for a complete lunch or dinner.

Scrambled Eggs with Mushrooms

Eggs are a staple breakfast protein. Scrambling is a healthier cooking method than frying because the egg protein is not charred, which makes it harder to digest. However, a scrambled egg can sometimes be too plain and bland. Pan-frying mushrooms produces a savory umami taste, while Italian frying peppers (also known as cubanelles) have thinner walls than regular green bell peppers and are sweeter and milder in flavor. Adding just these two ingredients will make this simple dish tastier and more interesting. Nonvegetarians could also add a touch of anchovy paste while pan-frying the mushrooms to bring additional complexity of flavor.

Preparation time: ⑤ minutes
Cooking time: ⑤ minutes
Serves: ④
For nut-free, use truffle oil

* 4 tablespoons olive oil
* ½ cup (50 g) coarsely chopped white mushrooms
* 8 eggs, at room temperature
* ¼ teaspoon coarse sea salt
* 5 drops toasted sesame oil or truffle oil
* 1 teaspoon cornstarch (cornflour) dissolved in 1 tablespoon water (optional; see *Note*)
* 2 Italian frying peppers (cubanelles), diced (optional)

1. In a large frying pan, heat 2 tablespoons of the olive oil over medium heat. Add the mushrooms and cook, stirring occasionally, until browned on all sides, 2–3 minutes.

2. While the mushrooms cook, beat the eggs thoroughly in a large bowl with the salt, sesame oil, and cornstarch (if using).

3. Once the mushrooms have browned, add the remaining 2 tablespoons oil to the pan. Wait 30 seconds and pour in the egg mixture. Stir constantly if you like the egg pillowy (my preference). Or let cook for 1–2 minutes without stirring if you like the egg firm. In that case, push the set egg to one side of the pan and let the liquid part cover the bottom. Repeat until most of the egg is set.

4. If using diced peppers, when the egg is almost set, stir them in. Transfer the eggs to a plate. The egg will continue to cook a little off the heat.

Note: If you like your eggs softer and more pillowy, add a little dissolved cornstarch before whisking. Start stirring right after adding the egg to the pan and don't stop until all the egg is almost set.

Variation: Instead of Italian frying peppers, try diced cucumber, peeled or unpeeled, to give this dish a refreshing taste. Use Persian (mini) cucumber, English (seedless) cucumber, or Asian cucumber, which has thinner skin and is less watery than the more common slicing cucumber when cooked.

> → *Pairs with* ←
> A hot cereal, toast, granola, or a pancake, plus ② servings of fresh fruit, for a complete breakfast. Pair with any salad or vegetable dish, plus a grain dish, for a complete lunch or dinner.

Boiled or Poached Eggs

Eggs are nutrient-dense and nutrient-balanced, an almost "perfect" food. They contain all of the ingredients, including all micronutrients, for a life to form. For many years, there have been concerns around the effect of eggs on cardiovascular health because they are high in cholesterol. More recent research shows that saturated fats rather than cholesterol are the culprit, and while eggs, along with shrimp (prawns), are high in cholesterol, they are low in saturated fat. Boiling or poaching eggs preserves the nutrients without adding extra fat, oil, or carbohydrates, and can serve as a fallback plan for your breakfast protein requirement when there is little time or you're looking for something simple.

Preparation time: ⑤ minutes
Cooking time: ③–⑨ minutes, according to method and preference
Serves: ④

* 8 eggs, at room temperature
* 1 tablespoon distilled white vinegar or apple cider vinegar (if poaching the eggs)

For boiled eggs:

1. Place the eggs in a medium pot with water to cover. Bring to a boil and start your timer. Simmer, covered, for your preferred length of time (see *Note*).

2. Place a large bowl under cold running tap water. Remove the eggs to the bowl to chill quickly, until you can hold the eggs in your hand. This will stop the cooking process and help separate the shell and membrane from the egg for easy peeling.

For poached eggs:

1. Set up a large bowl of ice and water.

2. Fill a large shallow pot with about 4 inches (10 cm) of water and bring to a boil. A large pot means the eggs can be spread out and thus prevent the water from cooling too quickly when they are added. Add the vinegar, which will help coagulate the egg white and reduce foam. Reduce the heat to a bare simmer (a few new bubbles keep forming at the bottom, but there is no rolling water to break up the egg white).

3. Crack an egg into a small cup or bowl.

4. Lower the cup as close to the simmering water as possible and gently slide the egg into the water, taking care not to splash. If you are making only a couple of poached eggs, you can swirl the hot water into a vortex and lower the eggs, one at a time, into the center of the vortex. This keeps the egg white centered around the yolk and results in a nice round shape for the poached eggs. The large diameter of the pot and the large amount of water help sustain the momentum of the swirling water and result in a rounder egg.

5. Simmer until the egg white is set but the yolk is still runny, 3–4 minutes. (To find just the right level of doneness, experiment as described in the *Note* below for boiled eggs.)

6. Remove the eggs with a spoon and place them in the cold water for only 1–2 minutes, just to stop the cooking process. They should be just warm to the touch. Serve, taking care to leave behind any debris.

Note: The time needed to boil eggs can vary, depending on the power of your burners, the water-to-egg ratio, the starting temperature of the eggs (room temperature versus fresh out of the refrigerator), size of the eggs, age of the eggs, and even the source. The best way to find the boiled egg you like is to do a trial and then stick with those parameters. Boil eggs as described above. Put 6 eggs into the water at once and set a timer. Remove an egg at 4, 5, 6, 7, 8, and 9 minutes respectively and chill the eggs as described in the recipe. Peel the eggs and find the time you like in your own kitchen with your own equipment. If you like very hard-boiled eggs, simmer them for 15 minutes.

> → *Pairs with* ←
> A hot cereal or toast, plus ② servings of fresh fruit, for a complete breakfast. Pair with any salad or vegetable dish, plus a grain dish, for a complete lunch or dinner.

Steamed Egg Custard

Eggs prepared this way are very soft, and easy to swallow and digest, ideal for anyone recovering from an illness. You can alter the firmness by adjusting the amount of water added. The ratio listed in the recipe will give you a firm consistency, similar to firm tofu. Using 2 cups (16 fl oz/475 ml) water will give the custard a softer, flan-like consistency; 2½ cups (18 fl oz/550 ml) will give it a consistency similar to silken/soft tofu. Covering the bowl tightly with plastic wrap (cling film) prevents the air trapped in the egg liquid from forming bubbles and results in a smoother consistency and mouthfeel.

Preparation time: ⑤ minutes
Cooking time: ①⑤ minutes
Serves: ④
For gluten-free, use gluten-free tamari

* 6 eggs, at room temperature
* 1 scallion (spring onion), chopped
* 1 white mushroom, chopped
* 5 drops toasted sesame oil
* 1 tablespoon soy sauce or gluten-free tamari
* Fine sea salt

1. Prepare a steamer fitted with a rack.

2. In a large heatproof bowl, beat the eggs thoroughly. Add 1½ cups (12 fl oz/350 ml) room-temperature water, the scallion (spring onion), and mushroom. Beat again to mix the ingredients well.

3. Cover the bowl tightly with plastic wrap (cling film). Place on the steamer rack and steam over boiling water until set in the center, about 15 minutes.

4. Remove the bowl and plastic wrap. Drizzle with the sesame oil and soy sauce, and season with salt to taste.

Variation: Replace the sesame oil with truffle oil for a change, and to make the recipe nut-free.

> → *Pairs with* ←
> A hot cereal, granola,
> or a pancake, plus ②
> servings of fresh fruit,
> for a complete breakfast.
> Pair with any salad or
> vegetable dish, plus a
> grain dish, for a complete
> lunch or dinner.

Silky Tofu with Dashi and Soy Sauce

It is common to eat soy products as a breakfast protein in East Asian countries. Soy is an almost perfect food; dried soybeans contain an ideal blend of macronutrients: roughly 35 percent protein, 20 percent fat, 30 percent carbohydrates, and 10 percent fiber. Four ounces (110 g) of soybeans will give you nearly all the vitamin B1, B2, folate, copper, magnesium, and manganese you need in a day. Soy protein is also balanced in amino acid compositions, almost like animal protein, so is invaluable for those on a vegan diet. Sources of breakfast protein in a Western diet often include eggs, meat, dairy, or fish, so soy and other beans are a good plant-based replacement. Tofu can be a little bland, so here dashi and soy sauce bring extra flavor.

Preparation time: ⑤ minutes, plus
① hour for the Dashi
Serves ④
For vegan/vegetarian dashi, see
Note 2

* 2 packets (14 oz/400 g) silken tofu
* 4 teaspoons soy sauce
* 4 teaspoons Dashi (see below)
* 1 scallion (spring onion), chopped

1. Rinse and drain the tofu. Cut each piece of tofu in half and put each half in a medium bowl. Cover with hot water for a few minutes to warm up, then drain. Alternatively, microwave each bowl on high for 1 minute or until heated through. Drain off any liquid that has seeped out.

2. Drizzle the soy sauce and dashi on top of the tofu. Top with chopped scallion (spring onion) and eat with a spoon.

Dashi

Dashi is a stock made from konbu (a kind of kelp seaweed) and flakes from dried bonito fish (katsuobushi—see *Note 1*). It is essential in Japanese cuisine, and many dishes rely on it to bring about the savory taste. It is equivalent to the chicken or vegetable stock used in Western cuisines. The ingredients for dashi can be found in Japanese or Asian grocery stores, and increasingly in the Asian food section of a supermarket. Or you can order online. If you can't find the ingredients, you can buy dashi powder (without MSG) and add water to reconstitute it.

Preparation time: ⑤ minutes, plus ③⓪ minutes' soaking time
Cooking time: ②⓪ minutes

* 1 piece dried konbu, about 4 × 8 inches (10 × 20 cm)
* 2 cups (30 g) dried bonito flakes (see *Note 2*)

1. Soak the konbu in 7½ cups (60 fl oz/ 1.75 liters) cold water in a medium saucepan for 30 minutes. Don't wash off the white powder on the konbu as it adds flavor to the dashi.

2. Bring the water to almost boiling. Turn off the heat and let the konbu sit for 5 minutes, then remove for other use (e.g., making a seaweed salad or miso soup). Do not boil the konbu, as it will bring out strong flavors that are unsuitable for making dashi.

3. Add the bonito flakes to the liquid. Bring to a boil, then reduce the heat and simmer, covered, for 5 minutes. Turn off the heat and let it sit for 10 minutes. Strain and store in the refrigerator for up to 2 days, or in the freezer for up to 1 month.

Note 1: To make katsuobushi, bonito fillets are fermented to produce intense umami flavors and then dried. The resulting dried fish is as hard as a piece of wood and can be shaved to produce the flakes.

Note 2: For a vegan/vegetarian version, replace the bonito flakes with dried shiitake mushrooms. Soak 4 medium dried shiitakes (½ oz/15 g) in cold water for 30 minutes. Slice thinly after soaking and cook in the same way as bonito flakes.

⇢ *Pairs with* ⇠
A hot cereal, plus ②
servings of fresh fruit, for a complete breakfast. Pair with a vegetable dish and a grain dish for a complete lunch or dinner.

Boiled Sweet Potato
with Refried Beans

Sweet potatoes have more fiber and beta-carotene (which gives them their yellow/orange color) than regular white potatoes, and are thus a healthier choice. However, they are still relatively starchy. The glycemic index can vary, depending on the cooking method: Boiled sweet potato is around 50 (medium), while a baked sweet potato can range from 60 to 90 (medium to high), because boiling preserves the better starch. In context, the glycemic index of boiled white potato is around 90 and baked white potatoes may even be higher than 100, because of the way the starch is structured. Boiling also softens the skin so you can eat it, and the skin is even more abundant in micronutrients than the flesh. Here, refried beans add protein and fiber, making it a healthier breakfast choice than other white potato-based breakfast dishes, such as hash browns or home fries. You can make refried beans from dried pinto beans, but it's a lot of work for breakfast, so I use canned beans here.

Preparation time: ①⓪ minutes
Cooking time: ③⓪ minutes
Serves ④

* 4 medium sweet potatoes
* 2 tablespoons olive oil
* 2 cloves garlic, peeled and crushed
* ¼ teaspoon cumin seeds
* ½ teaspoon crushed chili flakes
* 2 cans (15.5 oz/440 g each) pinto beans, drained and liquid reserved
* Juice of ½ lime, plus wedges for serving
* Fine sea salt
* 2 tablespoons coarsely chopped cilantro (coriander) leaves, for garnish

1. Put the sweet potatoes in a large pot with cold water to cover by about 2 inches (5 cm). Bring to a boil over high heat. Reduce the heat to medium and simmer, covered, until fork-tender, 20–30 minutes. Drain, and cut each potato in half lengthwise.

2. While the sweet potatoes cook, in a large frying pan, heat the olive oil over medium heat. Add the garlic, cumin seeds, and chili flakes. Cook until fragrant, about 1 minute. Add the drained beans and lime juice. Cook for 2 minutes, stirring vigorously, until the lime juice is absorbed and the beans are heated through. Add the reserved liquid from the can. Stir to combine and simmer, uncovered, mashing the beans with a sturdy spatula against the bottom or side of the pan to your desired consistency (you're aiming for coarsely mashed potato), about 5 minutes. Add a splash of water if the beans are drying out too much. Season with salt to taste.

3. Place two sweet potato halves on each plate, with the refried beans alongside. Sprinkle the cilantro (coriander) on top and serve with lime wedges.

→ *Pairs with* ←
② servings of fresh fruit or a smoothie for a complete breakfast. Pair with any salad or vegetable dish for a complete lunch or dinner.

Salads

Full Spectrum Salad

A well-made salad contains all the nutrients you need and takes little time to prepare. A healthy salad should have vegetables, some protein, oil, and optional carbohydrates. Because the leaf, fruit, and root of a vegetable contain different nutrients, a little of each creates this "full spectrum" salad, with its complex profile of plant-based ingredients. I prefer to use olive oil, vinegar, and salt to season salads, rather than bottled salad dressings, and add herbs and spices for extra flavor. You can eat a different version of this salad every day of the week without it feeling repetitive.

Preparation time: ②◎ minutes
Serves ④
For vegan/vegetarian, choose the appropriate salad options; for gluten-free, use gluten-free tamari

* 6–8 cups (500 g) bite-size pieces of leafy vegetables, such as romaine lettuce, kale, spinach, or mesclun
* 1–2 cups (170 g) bite-size pieces of fruit vegetables, such as tomato, cucumber, zucchini (courgette), or avocado
* 1–2 cups (220 g) bite-size pieces of root vegetables, such as cooked beets (beetroot), carrots, radishes, or cooked turnip
* 1 cup (120 g) bite-size pieces of fresh fruit, such as apple, peach, orange, or fig
* ⅓ cup (50 g) raw or toasted nuts, such as pecans, walnuts, almonds, or cashews
* 6 oz (175 g) protein, such as hard-boiled egg, canned tuna, tofu, or cooked beans
* 1 tablespoon raw or toasted seeds, such as flaxseeds, sesame seeds, pumpkin seeds, or sunflower seeds
* 1–2 tablespoons balsamic vinegar or juice of ¼–½ lemon
* 2 tablespoons extra-virgin olive oil
* ½ teaspoon coarse sea salt
* 1 teaspoon chopped fresh herbs (optional), such as basil, chives, parsley, or cilantro (coriander)
* Pinch of ground spice (optional), such as peppercorn, allspice, cumin, or nutmeg
* Other flavourings (optional), such as soy sauce or gluten-free tamari, raw onions, or scallions (spring onions)

1. Put all the vegetables, fruits, nuts, proteins, and seeds in a large bowl (see *Notes*). Toss well.

2. Drizzle with vinegar and olive oil. Toss to evenly coat the salad with the dressing.

3. Sprinkle with the salt, and add your chosen flavorings, if desired. Toss well and serve.

Flavoring options

Adjust the choice of herbs, spices, or additional ingredients to give the salad a flavor profile:

For an Italian flavor: Use basil.

For a Middle Eastern flavor: Use cilantro (coriander) and cumin.

For an East Asian flavor: Use scallions (spring onions) and soy sauce or gluten-free tamari.

Note 1: Use the freshest ingredients you can find, as this is the most important factor to make your salad taste delicious.

Note 2: Make sure you wash and then dry the vegetables well (with a salad spinner or patted dry with paper towel) or the salad will become mushy.

> ⇢ *Pairs with* ⇠
> A protein dish (legumes, fish, or meat), a grain dish, and a vegetable dish for a complete meal. It can also serve as a stand-alone light lunch or dinner.

Caesar Salad

A classic Caesar salad is a real crowd-pleaser. Instead of buying store-bought dressing and croutons, make your own for a fresher and more flavorful dish. Here I use less cheese than a traditional recipe, but more lettuce (which is mostly water and fiber with very few calories) to make it even healthier. I also like to add the croutons after the lettuce and dressing have been mixed, to keep their crispiness. Anchovies can be salty, so I use less added salt here. And combined with the anchovy, the Parmigiano-Reggiano cheese gives this salad an intense umami taste.

Preparation time: ①⓪ minutes
Cooking time: ①⑤ minutes
Serves ④

For the croutons:
* 2 slices whole-wheat sourdough bread
* 1 clove garlic, peeled but whole
* 1 tablespoon extra-virgin olive oil
* Pinch of fine sea salt
* Pinch of freshly ground black pepper

For the dressing:
* 2 egg yolks
* 4 oil-packed anchovy fillets, drained, or 2 teaspoons anchovy paste
* 2 tablespoons fresh lemon juice
* 1 clove garlic, peeled and crushed
* ¼ teaspoon fine sea salt
* ¼ teaspoon mustard powder
* ¼ teaspoon sugar
* 3 tablespoons extra-virgin olive oil

For the salad:
* 3 medium romaine lettuce hearts (about 12 oz/350 g total), cut into 1–2-inch (2.5–5 cm) pieces
* ¼ cup (20 g) freshly grated Parmigiano-Reggiano cheese

Make the croutons:
1. Preheat the oven to 350°F (180°C/Gas Mark 4).

2. Toast the bread in the oven so the surface hardens but is not browned, 3–5 minutes. Rub with the garlic, using the toasted surface as a grater. Chop any remaining garlic.

3. Cut or tear the bread into ½-inch (1.25 cm) cubes and place on a baking sheet. Sprinkle with the olive oil, chopped garlic, salt, and pepper. Toss evenly and spread out in a single layer so the bread cubes are not touching each other. Toast until browned and crispy, 10–15 minutes. Remove and let cool.

Make the dressing:
4. In a large coffee mug or spouted measuring cup (jug), combine the egg yolks, anchovy, lemon juice, garlic, salt, mustard powder, sugar, and 3 tablespoons water. Blend with a hand blender until smooth. Drizzle the olive oil slowly into the mixture while blending to emulsify. (You can also use a regular blender or mini food processor, but the small amount of ingredients may make blending a little hard.)

Assemble the salad:
5. In a large salad bowl, combine the lettuce and dressing and toss well. Sprinkle with the Parmigiano and croutons.

> → *Pairs with* ←
> A protein dish (legumes, fish, or meat) for a complete meal.

Chunky Cucumber Salad with Tomato and Feta

This is a version of a Greek salad. Instead of peeled and chopped regular cucumbers, I use unpeeled English (seedless) cucumbers or Persian (mini) cucumbers; the skin contains many beneficial nutrients and should be left on. Before cutting the cucumbers into chunks, I smash them slightly with the side of a kitchen knife or cleaver to break the cells and release more flavor. Use plum tomatoes here as they hold their shape. Crushing and grinding your own mustard seeds, instead of using ground mustard, gives the dish a more complex flavor. Feta cheese is made from sheep or goat's milk, both of which have a different nutrient profile from cow's milk. Feta can be quite salty, so a little goes a long way.

Preparation time: ①⑤ minutes
Serves ④

* ½ teaspoon mustard seeds
* ¼ teaspoon black peppercorns
* 1 teaspoon dried oregano
* 1 tablespoon red or white wine vinegar
* 1 tablespoon white wine
* 2 cloves garlic, minced
* 2 tablespoons extra-virgin olive oil
* 2 English (seedless) cucumbers or 6 Persian (mini) cucumbers (about 1 lb 8 oz/680 g total)
* 4 medium plum tomatoes, cut into 1-inch (2.5 cm) chunks
* 1 cup (200 g) cubed feta cheese
* ½ cup (75 g) pitted black olives
* Coarse sea salt

1. In a mortar and pestle (or a small spice grinder), crush and coarsely grind the mustard seeds, peppercorns, and oregano. (Or just crush them with a heavy pan on a cutting board.) Add to a small bowl with the vinegar, wine, garlic, and olive oil. Mix well and let sit for 10 minutes.

2. Meanwhile, cut off the ends of the cucumbers and wrap the cucumbers loosely with plastic wrap (cling film). Lay a cucumber flat on a cutting board and hit it lightly with the side of a large knife. (A cleaver works best because of its weight, or a kitchen mallet if you have one.) The force should be enough to crack the cucumbers open but not so much that they become mushy. Unwrap and cut the cucumbers into 1-inch (2.5 cm) chunks.

3. In a salad bowl, combine the cucumbers, tomatoes, feta, and olives and toss evenly. Beat the dressing and pour on top of the salad. Season to taste with salt, toss again, and serve.

> ⇾ *Pairs with* ⇽
> A protein dish (legumes, fish, or meat), a grain dish, and a vegetable dish for a complete meal. It can also serve as a stand-alone light lunch or dinner.

Roasted Beet and Radicchio Salad with Pine Nuts

Beet (beetroot) and radicchio are full of red pigments, which are antioxidants that scavenge the free radicals that create wear and tear on the cells and speed up aging. The sweetness of beet should be balanced by something slightly bitter, and radicchio makes a very good partner. Roasting mellows the flavors, and pine nuts add some creaminess to the mouthfeel. Radicchio is high in vitamin K, which is good for the blood and strong bones.

Preparation time: ⑤ minutes
Cooking time: ① hour
Serves ④

* 2 medium beets (beetroot), about 1 lb (450 g) total, peeled and cut into 1-inch (2.5 cm) chunks
* 1 lb (450 g) Treviso radicchio (or round Chioggia radicchio if not available), quartered through the stem
* 2 tablespoons extra-virgin olive oil
* ¼ teaspoon coarse sea salt
* ¼ cup (40 g) pine nuts
* Dash of truffle oil

1. Preheat the oven to 350°F (180°C/ Gas Mark 4).

2. Place the beets (beetroot) in a 9 × 13-inch (23 × 33 cm) glass baking dish and cover with foil. Roast until tender, 35–45 minutes. Let cool. Leave the oven on.

3. Line a baking sheet with parchment paper. Place the radicchio on one side of the sheet and brush with 1 tablespoon of the olive oil. Sprinkle with the salt. Spread the pine nuts on the other side of the baking sheet. Roast until the radicchio is lightly charred and the pine nuts are golden, about 10 minutes. Let cool.

4. In a serving bowl, combine the beets, radicchio, the remaining 1 tablespoon olive oil, and the pine nuts. Add the truffle oil and toss evenly.

> → *Pairs with* ←
> A protein dish (legumes, fish, or meat), a grain dish, and a vegetable dish for a complete meal. It can also serve as a stand-alone light lunch or dinner.

Grilled Portobello Mushroom and Eggplant Salad

Portobello mushrooms are very substantial and have an earthy and meaty taste, making them a good vegetarian substitute for beef. Here, I use them in a salad with grilled eggplant (aubergine), which also offers smoky and savory flavors. The cornstarch (cornflour) forms a nice crust when cooked, giving the mushroom caps a crunchy texture on the surface. Use a grill pan (griddle pan) if you have one, to get attractive grill marks on the mushrooms. Balance the mushrooms with some fresh leaves of frisée or spring mesclun, and the sweetness of apple strips, then finish with a few drops of truffle oil for a hearty and savory salad.

Preparation time: 25 minutes
Cooking time: 10 minutes
Serves 4
For vegan/vegetarian, use soy sauce or tamari; for gluten-free, use gluten-free tamari

* 1 tablespoon Worcestershire sauce, soy sauce, or gluten-free tamari
* 1 tablespoon balsamic vinegar
* 4 tablespoons olive oil
* 1 teaspoon finely chopped rosemary
* 2 teaspoons cornstarch (cornflour)
* 4 large portobello mushroom caps, stems removed and gills scraped out
* 4 slices eggplant (aubergine), each about ¾ inch (2 cm) thick
* ¼ teaspoon kosher (flaked) salt, if not using soy sauce
* 1 head frisée (about 1 lb/450 g), trimmed and torn into 1-inch (2.5 cm) pieces, or 8 oz (225 g) mesclun
* 1 apple, sliced into strips ¼ inch (6 mm) thick
* Pinch of freshly ground black pepper
* ½ teaspoon truffle oil

1. Place a large cast-iron skillet or grill pan (griddle pan) in the oven and preheat to 400°F (200°C/Gas Mark 6).

2. In a 9 × 13-inch (23 × 33 cm) baking dish, whisk together the Worcestershire sauce, vinegar, 1 tablespoon of the olive oil, the rosemary, and cornstarch (cornflour). Turn the mushroom caps to coat both sides in the marinade. Leave to marinate at room temperature for 15 minutes. Drain and pat dry.

3. Brush the eggplant (aubergine) slices with 1 tablespoon of the olive oil. Sprinkle with the salt and set aside on a plate.

4. Brush the skillet or grill pan with 1 tablespoon of the olive oil and brush the remaining 1 tablespoon olive oil onto the gill side of the mushroom caps. Place the caps in the skillet, gill-side up. Place the eggplant slices in the skillet as well. Roast until the mushroom tops are slightly tender, about 5 minutes. Flip the mushroom caps and the eggplant slices and roast until the second side is lightly browned, about 5 minutes more.

5. Divide the frisée and apple strips among four plates. Place one cooked mushroom cap and one eggplant slice on top of each. Sprinkle with pepper and truffle oil and serve.

Note: Grilled portobello mushrooms can be used to make a veggie burger. If you crave a cheeseburger but don't want to eat meat, fill the mushroom cup with cheese and assemble a burger as if it were the ground beef patty.

> → *Pairs with* ←
> A protein dish (legumes, fish, or meat), a grain dish, and a vegetable dish for a complete meal.

Salade Niçoise

This salad from the French Mediterranean coast (and the city of Nice) differs from other salads in that the ingredients are not tossed together but arranged separately on a plate. This kind of composed salad lets us appreciate the special flavors of each ingredient. Key players here are tuna and the black Niçoise olives, plus typical Provençal herbs, giving this salad its signature taste. It has a higher protein content than many other salads and can serve as a complete low-carbohydrate light dinner.

Preparation time: ①⑤ minutes
Cooking time: ①⓪ minutes
Serves ④

* 4 eggs, at room temperature

For the dressing:
* 2–3 tablespoons oil from canned tuna used in the salad
* 1 tablespoon extra-virgin olive oil
* 2 tablespoons red wine vinegar
* 1 clove garlic, minced
* 1 teaspoon dried herbes de Provence
* ¼ teaspoon kosher (flaked) salt
* Pinch of freshly ground black pepper (optional)

For the salad:
* 6–8 oz (175–225 g) mesclun
* 4 medium tomatoes, cut into wedges
* 1 English (seedless) cucumber, thickly sliced
* 1 small red onion, thinly sliced
* 1 yellow bell pepper, julienned
* 1 green bell pepper, julienned
* 8 oz (225 g) canned tuna in olive oil, drained and oil reserved for the dressing
* ½ cup (90 g) Niçoise olives, pitted

1. Put the eggs in a small saucepan with cold water to cover. Bring to a boil and reduce the heat to low, then cover and simmer for 10 minutes. Chill with cold water or running tap water. Peel and quarter lengthwise.

Make the dressing:
2. In a screw-top jar, combine the tuna oil, olive oil, vinegar, garlic, herbes de Provence, salt, and pepper (if using). Shake vigorously to make a smooth dressing.

Assemble the salad:
3. Prepare a bed of mesclun on each serving plate. Arrange the eggs, tomato, cucumber, red onion, bell peppers, tuna, and olives over the top. Feel free to be creative and make it attractive—you can arrange in rings or group each kind of ingredient together. Right before serving, shake the dressing again and drizzle over the top.

> ⇥ *Pairs with* ⇤
> A grain dish and a
> vegetable dish for a
> complete meal. It can also
> serve as a stand-alone
> light lunch or dinner.

Watercress Salad with Clementines and Wild Rice

Watercress is a cruciferous vegetable. It has a peppery taste, which, when combined and balanced with the sweetness of the clementines and the nuttiness of the hazelnuts, makes a lively salad that stimulates the palate. The wild rice here harmonizes everything. Although called "wild rice," it is neither wild nor a rice; it is the seed of a grass that is a botanical cousin to rice. What we get from the supermarket is cultivated, not grown wild. "Wild rice" has less starch than regular rice, with more protein and fiber and a chewier texture, perfect for this dish.

Preparation time: ①⑤ minutes
Cooking time: ① hour
Serves ④
For gluten-free, use gluten-free tamari

For the rice:
* ½ cup (90 g) wild rice, rinsed and drained
* 1½ cups (12 fl oz/350 ml) vegetable stock or water, plus more if needed
* ¼ teaspoon salt (optional; not needed if using vegetable stock)

For the nuts:
* ½ cup (75 g) skinned hazelnuts
* ½ cup (75 g) skin-on almonds
* 1 tablespoon avocado oil
* 1 teaspoon sugar
* 1 teaspoon honey
* ½ teaspoon kosher (flaked) salt

For the dressing:
* 1 tablespoon grated fresh ginger
* 1 tablespoon soy sauce or gluten-free tamari
* 2 tablespoons rice vinegar
* 1 teaspoon honey
* 2 tablespoons canola (rapeseed) oil, or any other neutral oil
* ½ teaspoon kosher (flaked) salt

For assembly:
* 1 lb (450 g) watercress, rinsed, tough ends trimmed, cut into pieces 1–2-inches (2.5–5 cm) long
* 4 clementines, halved and separated into segments
* Coarse sea salt (optional)

Make the rice:
1. In a medium saucepan, combine the rice, stock or water, and salt (if not using stock). Bring to a boil, then reduce to a simmer, cover, and cook over low heat until about half of the rice grains have burst open, 40–60 minutes, depending on the brand. (Don't uncover to check until 30 minutes—then add a little more stock or water if the pot seems dry.) Drain off any excess liquid and spread the cooked rice on a serving platter and let cool to room temperature.

Prepare the nuts:
2. While the rice is cooking, preheat the oven to 350°F (180°C/Gas Mark 4).

3. In a small bowl, combine the hazelnuts, almonds, avocado oil, sugar, honey, and salt and mix well to coat the nuts evenly. Spread the nuts on a baking sheet in a single layer, not touching each other. Roast until golden and fragrant, about 10 minutes, shaking the baking sheet midway through. (Watch them carefully: Hazelnuts burn easily.) Remove and let cool to room temperature, about 10 minutes.

Make the dressing:
4. In a bowl, combine the ginger, soy sauce, vinegar, honey, canola (rapeseed) oil, and salt and whisk well to form an emulsion.

Assemble the salad:
5. Scatter the watercress and clementine segments on top of the rice. Drizzle with the dressing and top with the toasted nuts. Sprinkle with coarse sea salt to taste, if desired.

> → *Pairs with* ←
> A protein dish (legumes, fish, or meat), a grain dish, and a vegetable dish for a complete meal. It can also serve as a stand-alone light lunch or dinner.

Guacamole Salad

Avocado is a good source of healthy oil. It is quite filling, making it easier to feel full without overeating. This salad is inspired by guacamole, and only takes a few easy steps to make. No fine dicing or mashing is needed and you get a chunkier texture than traditional guacamole. It is perfect as a salad instead of as a dip, skipping the fried tortilla chips that usually go with it. This is a dish with intense flavors and tastes— a combination of creaminess, sourness, saltiness, savoriness, and pungency. Store-bought guacamole is often not very fresh, so do give this version a go.

Preparation time: ①⓪ minutes
Serves ④

* 4 medium Hass avocados, cut into ½-inch (1.25 cm) chunks
* 2 small red onions, chopped
* 2 large heirloom tomatoes, cut into ½-inch (1.25 cm) chunks (see *Note 1*)
* 2 jalapeños, seeded and chopped (optional)
* ½ teaspoon coarse sea salt (see *Note 2*)
* 1 lime, halved, plus wedges for serving
* 3½ oz (100 g) cilantro (coriander), coarsely chopped

1. In a large bowl, gently combine the avocados, onions, tomatoes, and jalapeños (if using). Sprinkle with the salt. Squeeze the juice of the lime halves evenly over the salad. Top with the cilantro (coriander), toss, and serve with lime wedges.

Note 1: Never refrigerate tomatoes, as even a short exposure to refrigeration will make a tomato lose its fragrant flavor.

Note 2: Use coarse salt rather than fine salt for a salad like this. The larger salt grains will melt on the tongue and enhance the intensity of this dish.

> ⇻ *Pairs with* ⇺
> A protein dish (legumes, fish, or meat), a grain dish, and a vegetable dish for a complete meal. It can also serve as a stand-alone no-carbohydrate light dinner.

Arugula Salad with Walnuts and Shrimp

Arugula (also known as rocket or rucola) is a cruciferous vegetable with a hint of bitter, peppery flavor. It is balanced in this dish by the slight sweetness from the toasted walnuts. Shrimp (prawns) provide high-quality protein to round out a healthy and balanced dish.

Preparation time: ⑤ minutes
Cooking time: ②⓪ minutes
Serves ④

For the walnuts:
* 1 cup (150 g) walnuts
* 1 tablespoon honey
* 1 teaspoon sugar
* 1 teaspoon olive oil
* Pinch of ground cinnamon
* Pinch of fine sea salt

For the shrimp:
* 8 jumbo shrimp (prawns), peeled and deveined
* 1 teaspoon white wine
* ¼ teaspoon kosher (flaked) salt
* ¼ teaspoon cornstarch (cornflour)

For the salad:
* 2 cups (250 g) wild arugula (rocket), washed and trimmed
* Dash of truffle oil
* 2 tablespoons extra-virgin olive oil
* Juice of ¼ lemon, plus grated lemon zest for garnish and wedges for serving (optional)
* ¼ teaspoon coarse sea salt
* Garnish: 1 tablespoon pomegranate seeds, dried cranberries, or dried goji berries (optional)

Prepare the walnuts:

1. Preheat the oven to 350°F (180°C/Gas Mark 4). Line a baking sheet with parchment paper.

2. In a small bowl, toss the walnuts, honey, sugar, olive oil, cinnamon, and salt. Let sit for 5 minutes. Mix and spread on the lined baking sheet and bake until lightly browned, about 10 minutes. Remove and let cool until the walnuts are crispy.

Prepare the shrimp:

3. In a medium bowl, combine the shrimp (prawns), wine, salt, and cornstarch (cornflour). Let marinate for 5 minutes.

4. Meanwhile, bring 8 cups (64 fl oz/1.8 liters) water to boil in a medium saucepan. Add the shrimp to the hot water all at once so the starch seals them. Blanch until the shrimp become solidly opaque, 1–2 minutes, taking care not to overcook them. Drain well and refrigerate to chill for a few minutes.

Assemble the salad:

5. In a salad bowl, toss the arugula (rocket), walnuts, shrimp, truffle oil, extra-virgin olive oil, lemon juice, and salt and sprinkle with a little lemon zest. If desired, garnish with pomegranate seeds, dried cranberries, or dried goji berries, and serve with lemon wedges.

> → *Pairs with* ←
> A protein dish (legumes, fish, or meat), a grain dish, and a vegetable dish for a complete meal. It can also serve as a stand-alone light lunch or dinner.

Radish, Cucumber, and Dill Salad with Sour Cream

Radishes come in a variety of colors—white, green, yellow, red, and even purple. They belong to the cruciferous vegetable family. Those used most in salads are the small, round, red "summer" radishes, which have a sharp flavor. If the radishes have nice tops, don't discard them as they can also be eaten. Cook the radish tops like collards or other greens: sautéed, braised, or in soups. The sharp flavors of the radish are countered here by the refreshing cucumber and the creaminess of the sour cream. Dill adds the final layer of flavor. Radish, cucumber, and dill have very little fat, protein, or carbohydrates, so even with a little sour cream, this is still a low-calorie dish.

Preparation time: 10 minutes
Serves 4

* 16 red radishes, trimmed and thinly sliced
* 2 English (seedless) cucumbers, sliced into rounds ¼ inch (6 mm) thick
* 2 tablespoons chopped dill
* ½ cup (140 g) sour cream or whole-milk yogurt
* ½ teaspoon sugar
* Kosher (flaked) salt

1. In a large salad bowl, combine the radishes and cucumbers. Sprinkle with a ½ teaspoon salt and mix well. Let sit for 10 minutes. This will extract some moisture from the vegetables and make them crunchier.

2. Pour off any liquid collected in the bowl. Add the dill, sour cream, and sugar. Mix well and season to taste with salt. Serve right away so the vegetables stay crunchy.

> → Pairs with ←
> A protein dish (legumes, fish, or meat), a grain dish, and a vegetable dish for a complete meal.

Red Cabbage Coleslaw

The color of red cabbage comes from anthocyanins, a group of pigments with antioxidant properties. Cabbage is a cruciferous vegetable with all the health benefits of that class of vegetable, including reducing the risk of cancer. I have also added green cabbage and carrots to create variety in color. Coleslaw is usually made with mayonnaise, though here I make a homemade aioli for its garlicky taste and the fragrance offered by extra-virgin olive oil. It can also be made with only vinegar and oil, without using egg yolk.

Preparation time: ①⑤ minutes
Serves ④

For the aioli:
* 2 egg yolks
* 2 tablespoons extra-virgin olive oil
* 2 cloves garlic, peeled
* 1 teaspoon mustard seeds
* Pinch of celery seeds (optional)
* ½ teaspoon kosher (flaked) salt
* Juice of 1 lemon

For the salad:
* ½ medium head red cabbage (about 1 lb/450 g), thinly sliced
* ½ medium head regular cabbage (about 1 lb/450 g), thinly sliced
* 1 medium carrot, peeled and cut into matchsticks
* 1 tablespoon extra-virgin olive oil
* Kosher (flaked) salt
* Pinch of freshly ground black pepper

Make the aioli:
1. In a bowl, whisk the egg yolks and olive oil together. In a mortar and pestle (or a spice grinder), mash the garlic, mustard seeds, and celery seeds (if using).

2. Combine the ground spice mixture, salt, and lemon juice with the egg yolk/olive oil mixture. Whisk vigorously until emulsified.

Assemble the salad:
3. In a large bowl, combine both cabbages, the carrot, and aioli and toss evenly. Drizzle with the olive oil, then season with salt and pepper to taste. Toss again and serve.

Variation: To serve with vinaigrette: In a large bowl, vigorously whisk ¼ cup (2 fl oz/60 ml) each extra-virgin olive oil and distilled white vinegar or wine vinegar, ½ teaspoon sugar, 1 teaspoon ground mustard, and a pinch of ground celery seeds (optional). Assemble the salad as described, omitting the aioli and the olive oil, and toss with the vinaigrette.

> → *Pairs with* ←
> A protein dish (legumes, fish, or meat), a grain dish, and a vegetable dish for a complete meal.

Tabbouleh

Parsley is often used as a flavoring or garnish, but in tabbouleh (tabouli) it is the main player. This eastern Mediterranean salad is made of a generous amount of chopped parsley, mixed with tomato and bulgur. The parsley should be chopped finely, almost the same size as the bulgur. I like to use a cleaver for this, as the weight makes the repeated chopping movements a lot easier than a chef's knife. You can also use a food processor, but make sure the blade is very sharp to get the clean cut and so the parsley doesn't become watery. Bulgur is a low glycemic index wheat product and is a whole grain with a pleasant nutty taste.

Preparation time: 20 minutes, plus 30 minutes' soaking time
Serves 4

* 1 cup (170 g) extra-fine grain bulgur
* 2 cups (16 fl oz/475 ml) boiling water
* 4 cups (240 g) very finely chopped flat-leaf parsley (see *Note*)
* 4 plum tomatoes, finely chopped
* Juice of ½ lemon, plus wedges for serving
* 2 tablespoons extra-virgin olive oil
* ½ teaspoon coarse sea salt
* Pinch of freshly ground black pepper

1. Put the bulgur in a large heatproof serving bowl and pour the boiling water over. Let sit, covered, for 15 minutes.

2. If any liquid remains, drain off as much as possible.

3. Return the bulgur to the bowl and add the parsley, tomatoes, lemon juice, olive oil, salt, and pepper. Toss well to combine and serve with lemon wedges.

Note: Before chopping the parsley, soak the leaves in cold water for 30 minutes or more ahead of time. This will help the parsley reabsorb the water lost during storage and result in a crunchier texture. In fact, if you can, presoak all vegetables in this manner before cooking. Since we can't always get vegetables fresh from the field, they inevitably lose moisture and wilt somewhat during storage, be it at room temperature or in a refrigerator. Presoaking rehydrates them and gives you plumper ingredients and better mouthfeel in your finished dish. For this dish, make sure you dry the parsley thoroughly before chopping so it doesn't end up soggy.

> → *Pairs with* ←
> A protein dish (legumes, fish, or meat), a grain dish, and a vegetable dish for a complete meal. It can also serve as a stand-alone light lunch or dinner.

Seaweed Salad with Miso and Sesame Seeds

Occasionally, change up your routine and use seaweed instead of leafy vegetables to make a salad. Seaweed is high in omega-3 fatty acids, iodine, and other minerals. Brown seaweed (kelp) contains fucoidan, a substance that helps the immune system. Here, I use both wakame (the thin green seaweed used in the traditional "seaweed salad" in Japanese restaurants in Western countries) and konbu (the large and thick brown-colored algae). They are available from Japanese or Asian grocery stores or online. Miso paste is made of fermented soybeans—the soy protein is broken down during the fermentation process, enhancing taste and easing digestion.

Preparation time: 20 minutes,
plus overnight marinating time
Serves 4
For vegan/vegetarian, see *Note 2*
of the Dashi recipe (page 68)

* 1 oz (25 g) dried green wakame
* 1 oz (25 g) dried brown konbu, thin
  (4 × 16 inches/10 × 40 cm) or thick
  (4 × 8 inches/10 × 20 cm)
* 2 oz (50 g) tofu sheet (optional;
  see *Note*)
* 2 scallions (spring onions),
  thinly sliced
* 1 medium carrot, shredded
* 2 teaspoons grated fresh ginger
* 2 tablespoons white miso
* 2 tablespoons rice vinegar
* 2 tablespoons Dashi (page 68)
  or water
* 1 teaspoon mirin
* 1 teaspoon toasted sesame oil
* ½ teaspoon coarse sea salt
* Pinch of freshly ground white
  pepper
* 1 teaspoon grated lemon zest
  (optional)
* 1 teaspoon toasted sesame seeds

1. Rehydrate the seaweeds (wakame and konbu) by soaking them in warm water for 10 minutes. Rinse and drain. Cut the seaweeds and the tofu sheet (if using) into very thin slices, about ⅛–¼-inch (3–6 mm) wide and less than 4 inches (10 cm) long. Transfer to a serving bowl.

2. Add the scallions (spring onions) and carrot to the seaweed mixture.

3. In a small bowl, combine the ginger, miso, vinegar, dashi, mirin, sesame oil, salt, white pepper, and lemon zest (if using) and whisk thoroughly to combine. Drizzle over the seaweed mixture and toss to combine. Let marinate at room temperature for about 15 minutes or overnight in the refrigerator.

4. Sprinkle with the sesame seeds ready for serving.

Note: A tofu sheet (also known as dried bean curd sheet) is tofu that has been compressed into a firm, crepe-like sheet.

→ *Pairs with* ←
A protein dish (legumes,
fish, or meat), a grain dish,
and a vegetable dish for a
complete meal.

Fennel Salad
with Fruit and Nuts

The main player in this salad is the fennel. Fennel has a refreshing and aromatic taste and a crunchy texture, but it needs other ingredients to balance those characteristics. It pairs well with something soft, fragrant, and with some fat content, such as fruits, nuts, cheese, or avocado, which has protein and fat nutrients. Fennel is also rich in fiber. This dish is a nice change from a typical leafy green salad. The banana provides a soft texture to balance the crispy fennel, and its sweetness and fragrance complement the fennel's anise-like taste.

Preparation time: ①⑤ minutes
Serves ④
For vegan and dairy-free, omit the cheese

* 2 fennel bulbs (about 8 oz/225 g each), thinly sliced, plus 1 table-spoon chopped tender fronds (or chopped dill)
* 2 red apples, sliced
* 1 banana, sliced
* 2 small Hass avocados, thickly sliced
* ½ cup (75 g) walnut halves
* ¼ cup (45 g) dried cranberries
* 2 tablespoons extra-virgin olive oil
* Juice of ½ lemon
* 1 tablespoon shaved firm cheese (optional), such as Manchego, Gruyère, Parmigiano-Reggiano, or Gouda
* Sea salt

1. In a large salad bowl, combine the fennel, apples, banana, avocados, walnuts, and cranberries and toss gently to combine.

2. Drizzle with the olive oil and lemon juice. Season with salt to taste and toss.

3. Divide among four serving plates. Sprinkle with the reserved fennel fronds and cheese (if using), and serve.

> → *Pairs with* ←
> A protein dish (legumes, fish, or meat), a grain dish, and a vegetable dish for a complete meal. It can also serve as a stand-alone light lunch or dinner.

Assorted Vegetables with Baba Ghanoush

Raw vegetables can be enjoyed with a nutritious dip. This Middle Eastern dish is made of eggplant (aubergine) and tahini. It has a pleasant smoky flavor and creamy texture. Tahini is full of good fat and protein. Once made, the baba ghanoush can be stored in the refrigerator for several days, making it handy to put together and have ready for a quick lunch or dinner. You can buy baba ghanoush, but a homemade one tastes fresher and more flavorful.

Preparation time: 20 minutes
Cooking time: 50 minutes
Serves 4

* 2 medium eggplants (aubergines), about 1 lb (450 g) each, halved lengthwise
* 4 tablespoons extra-virgin olive oil
* 3 cloves garlic, peeled
* ¼ teaspoon cumin seeds
* Pinch of cayenne pepper
* Juice of ½ lemon
* ½ teaspoon fine sea salt, plus extra for seasoning
* ½ cup (140 g) tahini
* 1 tablespoon chopped parsley
* Pinch of sweet paprika
* 1 teaspoon pomegranate seeds (optional), for garnish (eat the rest for dessert)
* 2 medium carrots, cut into sticks 3–4 inches (7.5–10 cm) long
* 1 red or green bell pepper, cut into sticks 3–4 inches (7.5–10 cm) long
* 1 zucchini (courgette), cut into sticks 3–4 inches (7.5–10 cm) long
* 1 small cucumber, cut into sticks 3–4 inches (7.5–10 cm) long
* 2 stalks celery, cut into sticks 3–4 inches (7.5–10 cm) long

1. Preheat the oven to 400°F (200°C/ Gas Mark 6). Line a baking sheet with parchment paper.

2. Arrange the eggplants (aubergines), cut-side up, on the lined baking sheet. Brush the cut sides with 1 tablespoon of the olive oil. Roast until the flesh becomes soft and collapsed and the surface lightly browned, 40–50 minutes.

3. Remove and let cool to room temperature. Scoop the flesh into a sieve and discard the skins. Press gently with the back of the spoon and let the extra liquid drain off.

4. In a mortar and pestle (or spice grinder), pound and grind the garlic, cumin seeds, and cayenne to a fine paste. Mix in the lemon juice. Scrape up the spice paste and transfer to a medium bowl.

5. Add the drained eggplant, 2 tablespoons of olive oil, the salt, tahini, and half the chopped parsley to the bowl. Mix vigorously with a fork to beat the mixture into a smooth paste. Add water to achieve the desired thickness, if needed. (You can also use a food processor.)

6. Season with more salt to taste. Drizzle with the remaining 1 tablespoon olive oil. Garnish with the remaining parsley, the paprika, and pomegranate seeds (if using). Serve with the vegetables.

> → *Pairs with* ←
> A grain dish and a
> vegetable dish for a
> complete meal.

Vegetables

Pan-Fried Asparagus

Asparagus pairs well with almost any protein dish. It has a unique taste and is rich in fiber. Here, I use a simple pan-fry method with only oil and salt, which is quick and retains the bright color of the asparagus. You may want to peel the white part of the stem to remove the fibrous skin, or just cut it off. The skin on the green part can be eaten.

Preparation time: ⑤ minutes
Cooking time: ①⓪ minutes
Serves ④

* 2 tablespoons extra-virgin olive oil
* 1 clove garlic, crushed with the side of a knife and peeled
* 1 bunch (about 1 lb/450 g) asparagus, white fibrous stem peeled or removed (see *Note*)
* ¼ teaspoon coarse sea salt

1. In a large frying pan, heat the olive oil over medium heat. Add the garlic and cook until lightly browned, about 1 minute. Remove the garlic.

2. Arrange the asparagus in a single layer in the pan, with the spears pointing in the same direction. Cook undisturbed over medium heat until lightly browned, about 5 minutes.

3. Turn the asparagus and cook, undisturbed, until the second side is browned and the asparagus is just tender and bright green, 3–5 minutes. Sprinkle the salt on top and shake the pan so the asparagus rolls a little and is coated evenly with salt.

Note: Asparagus should be sold with the stems standing up in water to keep them well hydrated. This may not always be the case in the supermarket, and it can be hard to store them like that at home. You can cut a thin slice from the base of the stems and soak the asparagus in cold water for 10 minutes before cooking, to help them absorb water and stay plump during the cooking process.

→ *Pairs with* ←
A protein dish (legumes, fish, or meat), a grain dish, and another vegetable or salad dish for a complete meal.

Peruvian Stuffed Peppers

I learned how to make this signature regional dish in a cooking class while visiting Arequipa, Peru. We used the very spicy ají rocoto—a largish lantern-shaped chili that is much hotter than a jalapeño. Here, I replace it with red bell pepper, which has a similar shape, is widely available, and not as challenging to eat. Instead of the traditional ground meat, I use hard-boiled eggs, lentils, and yogurt to give this vegetarian dish savory flavors.

Preparation time: ①⑤ minutes
Cooking time: ① hour
Serves ④

* 2 tablespoons olive oil
* ½ teaspoon fennel seeds
* ½ teaspoon caraway seeds
* ½ medium onion, chopped
* 2 cloves garlic, minced
* 1 cup (200 g) green or brown lentils, rinsed
* ¼–½ teaspoon cayenne pepper, depending on your taste for heat
* 2 cups (16 fl oz/475 ml) hot water
* 4 large red bell peppers
* 2 eggs, hard-boiled, peeled, and coarsely chopped
* ¼ cup (70 g) plain Greek yogurt
* 1 large plum tomato, chopped
* ¼ cup (25 g) grated Manchego cheese, or a vegetarian alternative
* Kosher (flaked) salt

1. Preheat the oven to 375°F (190°C/Gas Mark 5).

2. In a medium saucepan, heat the olive oil over medium heat. Add the fennel and caraway seeds and cook until fragrant, about 30 seconds. Add the onion and garlic and sweat over low heat until fragrant, about 3 minutes.

3. Increase the heat to high. Add the lentils and cayenne and let cook, undisturbed, for 2 minutes to fry the lentils a little. Stir once and cook for another 2 minutes, then add the hot water, cover, and simmer over low heat until the lentils are tender but not falling apart, about 20 minutes.

4. Slice off the top ½ inch (1.25 cm) of the bell peppers and set aside. Remove the seeds from the peppers.

5. Add the eggs, yogurt, and tomato to the lentils and mix well. Season with salt to taste. Stuff the mixture into the peppers, sprinkle with the Manchego, and set the lids on top.

6. Set the peppers in a baking dish that fits them snugly. Transfer to the oven and bake until the peppers are tender, 30–35 minutes.

Note: If you'd like the filling to have a crispy top, bake the pepper tops alongside the stuffed peppers, rather than on top.

⇥ *Pairs with* ⇤
A grain dish and another vegetable or salad dish for a complete meal.

Braised Leeks with Thyme

Leeks belong to the same plant family as onions and garlic. As such, they are fragrant and pair well with animal protein dishes, but they're milder than onions and garlic, so can serve as a stand-alone vegetable dish as well. Here, mushrooms and sun-dried tomatoes are added to bring complexity in flavor.

Preparation time: 10 minutes
Cooking time: 15 minutes
Serves 4

* 2 cups (16 fl oz/475 ml) water or vegetable stock
* 2 tablespoons extra-virgin olive oil
* 2 large leeks (about 8 oz/225 g each), thoroughly cleaned and cut into quarter-lengths (see *Note*)
* 4 cloves garlic, minced
* 1 sprig thyme
* 1 cup (90 g) sliced white mushrooms
* 1 tablespoon sun-dried tomatoes, roughly chopped
* Coarse sea salt

1. In a small pot, boil the water and set aside to cool slightly.

2. In a large frying pan, heat the olive oil over medium heat. Add the leek pieces, cut-side down, and cook until slightly browned, 2–3 minutes. Add the garlic, thyme, and mushroom slices to the spaces in the pan to brown them, too. Flip the leeks and brown the other side, about 2 minutes.

3. Add just enough hot water to cover (you may not need all of it), then add the sun-dried tomatoes. Simmer over low heat, uncovered, until the leeks are soft, 5–8 minutes.

4. Increase the heat to medium-high and cook for 2–3 minutes to reduce and thicken the juices. Season to taste with salt.

5. Plate the leeks and pour the pan juices over the top.

Note: After thoroughly cleaning the leeks, cut off the dark green tops so you're left with just the white and light-green portion. Halve each leek lengthwise, then halve each piece crosswise, resulting in four quarter-lengths per leek, eight pieces total.

> ⇥ *Pairs with* ⇤
> A protein dish (legumes, fish, or meat), a grain dish, and another vegetable or salad dish for a complete meal.

Roasted Brussels Sprouts with Rosemary

Brussels sprouts are cruciferous vegetables with special health benefits. Within this family of vegetables are kale, broccoli, cauliflower, collard greens, bok choy, watercress, arugula (rocket), radish, and various cabbages. These vegetables are very healthy for you and contain substances that help cancer prevention. Boiling reduces those substances, so the vegetables should be eaten raw, steamed, sautéed, stir-fried, or roasted. Roasting Brussels sprouts in the presence of rosemary enhances their flavor, and this vegetable dish pairs well with equally strong-flavored legume or meat protein dishes.

Preparation time: ①⓪ minutes
Cooking time: ②⓪ minutes
Serves ④

* 1 lb (450 g) Brussels sprouts, trimmed and halved lengthwise
* 2 tablespoons extra-virgin olive oil
* ½ teaspoon coarse sea salt
* 1 sprig rosemary, needles finely chopped

1. Preheat the oven to 400°F (200°C/ Gas Mark 6).

2. In a large bowl, combine the Brussels sprouts, olive oil, salt, and rosemary. Toss thoroughly.

3. Arrange the sprouts on a sheet pan, cutside down, leaving room in between. Roast until the outside leaves are browned and the inside is tender, 15–20 minutes.

Note: When roasting vegetables, coat with a thin layer of olive oil and spread them out on the baking sheet so they don't touch one another. If too crowded, the moisture generated during roasting will steam the vegetables, instead of the dry heat roasting them, leading to soggy vegetables. To make the outside crisp and the inside tender, use a higher temperature, but not so high as to burn the vegetables.

> → *Pairs with* ←
> A protein dish (legumes or meat), a grain dish, and another vegetable or salad dish for a complete meal.

Peppery Collard Greens with Tomato and Jalapeño

Collards are another cruciferous vegetable of high nutritional value, rich in dietary fiber and the vitamins A, C, and K. Green leafy vegetables should not be overcooked, so their nutrients are retained. Here, collard greens are sautéed with tomato to enhance the taste, and with black pepper, dried chili pepper, and fresh jalapeños to give the dish a spicy kick.

Preparation time: ⑤ minutes
Cooking time: ①⓪ minutes
Serves ④

* 3 tablespoons olive oil
* 4 dried red chilies with seeds, crumbled to small pieces (or crushed chili flakes, to taste)
* 4 cloves garlic, chopped
* 16 large cherry tomatoes, halved
* ½ teaspoon kosher (flaked) salt
* ¼ teaspoon freshly ground black pepper
* 1 lb (450 g) collard greens, stems removed and leaves sliced crosswise
* 2 jalapeños, seeded and chopped

1. In a large frying pan, heat the olive oil over medium heat. Add the dried chilies and garlic and cook until fragrant, about 1 minute.

2. Add the tomatoes, ¼ teaspoon of the salt, and the black pepper. Cook until the tomato is softened, about 3 minutes. Stir in the collard greens, cover, and cook until wilted, about 2 minutes. Stir once and continue to cook, covered, about 2 minutes more.

3. Add the jalapeños and remaining ¼ teaspoon salt, then stir and cook until the jalapeños are softened, about 1 minute.

> ⇢ *Pairs with* ⇠
> A protein dish (legumes, fish, or meat), a grain dish, and another vegetable or salad dish for a complete meal.

Steamed Kabocha Squash Bowl

Kabocha squash, or Japanese pumpkin, is much smaller than a traditional pumpkin and has a deep green skin. It has a chestnut-like taste and a hint of buttery fragrance, sweeter and less "vegetable-tasting" than other squash. People who don't like to eat vegetables might still enjoy kabocha squash, enabling them to meet their vegetable requirement in a meal. Kabocha can be roasted as other squash, but steaming it gives it a cleaner and purer taste. Steaming is also a healthier cooking method than roasting because the cooking temperature is lower, keeping the food moist and easier to digest. This is a healthy and delicate vegan dish, with the orange flesh of the squash rich in beta-carotene.

Preparation time: ①⓪ minutes
Cooking time: ①⑤ minutes
Serves ④

* 2 small kabocha squash (Japanese pumpkins), about 1 lb/450 g each
* 1 cup (160 g) shelled edamame or green peas
* 1 cup (170 g) dried pitted dates or jujubes (red dates)
* ¼ cup (10 g) unsweetened coconut flakes
* ¼ teaspoon kosher (flaked) salt
* 2 tablespoons coconut milk, cashew milk, or almond milk

1. In a large steamer pot (10 inches/25 cm in diameter or greater), bring 2 inches (5 cm) water to a simmer over high heat.

2. Cut each squash lengthwise (through the stem and blossom ends) in half. Scoop out the seeds to make bowls.

3. Divide the edamame, dates, and coconut flakes among the bowls. Sprinkle with the salt.

4. Once the water in the steamer boils, nestle the squash halves in the steamer insert, skin-side down. (You can tilt to the side a bit to make them fit, just don't let the filling spill out.) Cover and steam over medium to medium-high heat until tender, about 10 minutes. Transfer the squash bowls to a plate, drizzle the nut milk into the center of each, and serve.

Note: If you don't have a large-diameter steamer, you can use a Dutch oven (casserole) with a rack in the bottom.

> → *Pairs with* ←
> A protein dish (legumes, fish, or meat), a grain dish, and another vegetable or salad dish for a complete meal.

Cauliflower, Mushroom, and Sauerkraut Casserole

Casserole cooking seals the flavors of all the ingredients under a layer of crust, resulting in a very hearty and savory dish. Casseroles often contain meat, but here I use mushrooms instead to create a plant-based meal. Sauerkraut is made by fermenting cabbage with probiotics—microbes that also reside in our gut and contribute to our health. These microbes break down the carbohydrates and proteins in the cabbage to make them easier to digest. In the process, complex flavors are also generated, which add to the umami taste of the dish. This dish contains all the macronutrients and can serve as a complete light meal.

Preparation time: 10 minutes
Cooking time: 40 minutes
Serves 4

* 2 tablespoons extra-virgin olive oil
* ½ medium yellow onion, thinly sliced
* 2 cloves garlic, minced
* 1 lb (450 g) white or cremini (chestnut) mushrooms, thinly sliced
* 8 oz (225 g) sauerkraut, rinsed and drained well
* 2 bay leaves, fresh or dried
* 1 teaspoon sweet paprika
* Splash of fortified wine, such as Marsala or sherry
* ½ teaspoon kosher (flaked) salt
* Dash of freshly ground black pepper
* 1 small head cauliflower (about 2 lb/900 g), cut into florets
* 1 cup (50 g) panko breadcrumbs or other dried breadcrumbs
* ¾–1 cup (210–280 g) plain whole-milk yogurt

1. Preheat the oven to 375°F (190°C/Gas Mark 5).

2. In a large ovenproof frying pan, heat the olive oil over medium heat. Add the onion, garlic, and mushrooms and sauté until fragrant and the mushrooms are slightly browned, 3–4 minutes.

3. Add the sauerkraut, bay leaves, paprika, wine, salt, and pepper, and cook until you can smell the acidity of the wine, 1–2 minutes. Add about ½ cup (4 fl oz/120 ml) water and bring to a simmer to loosen the crusty bits in the bottom of the pan.

4. Stir in the cauliflower florets and bring to a simmer.

5. In a medium bowl, combine the panko breadcrumbs and ¾ cup (210 g) of the yogurt and work with your fingers or a fork until you have a thick, crumbly texture, adding up to ¼ cup (70 g) more yogurt if needed.

6. Flatten the top of the cauliflower mixture and top with the breadcrumbs.

7. Transfer the pan to the oven and bake, uncovered, until the cauliflower is tender, about 30 minutes. The top should be golden brown. If not, broil (grill) for a few minutes more.

⇢ *Pairs with* ⇠
A protein dish (legumes, fish, or meat) and another vegetable or salad dish for a complete meal. It can also serve as a stand-alone light lunch or dinner.

Salt and Vinegar Napa Cabbage

Napa cabbage (also known as Chinese cabbage, Chinese leaf, winter cabbage, or wombok) is a cruciferous vegetable popular in East Asia. In Korean cuisine it is pickled to make kimchi and used as a side dish at almost every meal. Napa cabbage contains the healthy substances found in other cruciferous vegetables. It is mild in taste and agreeable to those who may find other cruciferous vegetables slightly bitter. Ten ounces (280 g) of napa cabbage will give you the entire amount of vitamin C you need in a day.

Preparation time: 10 minutes
Cooking time: 10 minutes
Serves 4
For vegan/vegetarian, omit the
  dried shrimp

* 3 tablespoons olive oil
* 1 cup (90 g) sliced shiitake
  mushrooms
* 1 scallion (spring onion), chopped
* 1 teaspoon small dried shrimp
  (optional), each about ½ inch
  (1.25 cm) long (see *Note*)
* 1 head napa cabbage (Chinese leaf),
  about 2 lb (900 g), coarsely chopped
* 1–1½ tablespoons rice vinegar
  or distilled white vinegar
* ½ tablespoon sugar
* 2 cloves garlic, minced
* 1 tablespoon chopped fresh red
  chili (if spiciness is desired) or
  red bell pepper
* Coarse sea salt

1. In a wok or large, deep pan, heat the olive oil over medium heat. Add the mushrooms, scallion (spring onion), and dried shrimp (if using). Stir-fry until browned, about 2 minutes.

2. Increase the heat to high and add the cabbage, stirring constantly until softened, 2–3 minutes. Add the vinegar and sugar. Stir and cook for 2 minutes. (The cabbage will cook down significantly to about one-quarter the original volume.)

3. Remove from the heat. Stir in the garlic and chili. Season to taste with sea salt.

Note: In East Asian and Southeast Asian cuisine, dried shrimp are used to add umami to a dish like this. When tiny shrimp are dried slowly, a little bit of fermentation occurs during the process, similar to when fish sauce is being made. This breaks down the shrimp proteins to peptides and amino acids, although to a much lesser degree than fish sauce, meaning the resulting umami taste is more subtle and less pungent. If you can't find dried shrimp, dried anchovy or even anchovy paste can substitute for the same flavor.

> → *Pairs with* ←
> A protein dish (legumes,
> fish, or meat), a grain
> dish, and another
> vegetable or salad dish
> for a complete meal.

Pan-Fried King Oyster Mushrooms and Tofu

This is a vegan dish full of protein and flavor, as mushrooms contain substances rich in the savory umami taste. The cooking process brings out more of this taste, giving the dish a meaty flavor. King oyster mushrooms (also known as king trumpet mushrooms) are large and dense, which adds to the meatiness, making this dish appealing to vegans and carnivores alike. If king oyster mushrooms are not available, use another mushroom like portobello, sliced about ½ inch (1.25 cm) thick. Tofu is rich in healthy protein and calcium but can be bland in taste, so it benefits from being paired with the mushroom and other strong flavors like soy and allspice.

Preparation time: ①⑤ minutes
Cooking time: ①⑤ minutes
Serves ②
For gluten-free, use gluten-free tamari

* 8 oz (225 g) king oyster (king trumpet) mushrooms
* ½ teaspoon ground allspice, or other warm spice like cumin or coriander
* 14 oz (440 g) firm tofu, cut into slices ½ inch (1 cm) thick
* Kosher (flaked) salt and freshly ground black pepper
* 3 tablespoons extra-virgin olive oil
* 4 cups (120 g) loosely packed spinach leaves
* 1 teaspoon soy sauce or gluten-free tamari

1. Halve two of the mushrooms lengthwise. Slice the remaining mushrooms crosswise into disks ½ inch (1.25 cm) thick. (These cuts make them less chewy.) Score all the pieces on both sides with a shallow crisscross pattern to facilitate penetration of flavor. Rub the allspice on both sides of the mushrooms and tofu. Season to taste with salt and pepper.

2. In a large frying pan, heat 2 tablespoons of the olive oil over medium heat. Lay the mushrooms flat in the pan. Cook until the mushrooms wither a bit and the underside turns light brown, 2–3 minutes. Flip the mushroom pieces and repeat on the other side. Remove to a plate and set aside.

3. Add the remaining 1 tablespoon olive oil to the pan over medium heat. Add the tofu slices and brown on both sides, about 2 minutes per side. Remove to the plate with the mushrooms.

4. Add the spinach to the oil remaining in the pan. Cook over medium heat until it wilts, 3–5 minutes. Add the soy sauce and stir.

5. Arrange the cooked spinach on a serving platter. Layer the tofu and then the mushrooms on top. Pour the pan juices over the top and serve.

> ⇢ *Pairs with* ⇠
> A grain dish and another vegetable or salad dish for a complete meal.

Sautéed Kale with Cashews

Kale is a curly-leaved cultivar in the cabbage family. It has all the benefits of a cruciferous vegetable, and is also very high in vitamin K (good for your blood and bone strength) and high in lutein (good for your eyes), calcium (also for bone strength), and vitamins A and C. Cashews add a nutty flavor and crunchiness to complement the kale.

Preparation time: ⑤ minutes
Cooking time: ①⓪ minutes
Serves ④

* 1 cup (150 g) cashews
* 2 tablespoons olive oil
* 2 cloves garlic, minced
* 1 lb 8 oz (680 g) kale, stems removed and leaves roughly chopped
* 1 teaspoon sugar
* 1 teaspoon balsamic vinegar
* ¼ cup (2 fl oz/60 ml) water or vegetable stock
* ½ teaspoon coarse sea salt

1. Preheat the oven to 350°F (180°C/Gas Mark 4).

2. Spread the cashews on a baking sheet and toast until golden and crispy, about 5 minutes.

3. Meanwhile, in a large frying pan, heat the olive oil over medium heat. Add the garlic and cook until fragrant, 1–2 minutes.

4. Add the kale. Cook undisturbed to brown some of the leaves, about 1 minute. Add the sugar, vinegar, and water and stir to combine. Cook, covered, until the kale wilts and turns dark green, 5–7 minutes.

5. Season the kale with the salt, transfer to a serving dish, and top with the cashews.

> → *Pairs with* ←
> A protein dish (legumes, fish, or meat), a grain dish, and another vegetable or salad dish for a complete meal.

Sautéed Zucchini with Garlic

Zucchini (courgette) is a very versatile vegetable. It can be eaten raw, steamed, baked, grilled, sautéed, or cooked in stews and soups. It has a mild flavor and is not very fibrous, which is why I often recommend this dish to people who need something simple during recovery. Here I sauté, to keep it soft, and the only flavoring ingredients are garlic and lemon juice to preserve its delicate tones. Zucchini comes in various colors and shapes, the most common being the uniformly green variety. Try others if you can find them, and combine them in this dish.

Preparation time: ①◎ minutes
Cooking time: ①◎ minutes
Serves ④

* 2 tablespoons extra-virgin olive oil
* 4 zucchini (courgettes), about
  1¾ lb (800 g) total, cut into rounds
  ¼ inch (6 mm) thick
* ¼ teaspoon fine sea salt, plus extra
  for seasoning
* ¼–1 teaspoon crushed chili flakes,
  depending on desired heat
* Juice of ¼ lemon
* 4 cloves garlic, finely chopped

1. In a large frying pan, heat the olive oil over medium heat. When hot, add the zucchini (courgettes) and cook undisturbed until they soften a little and the underside is lightly browned, about 2 minutes.

2. Add the salt and chili flakes and toss to combine. Cook until the zucchini is tender, 2–3 minutes.

3. Add the lemon juice and garlic and toss again to combine. Cook until the acidity reduces, about 1 minute. Season to taste with additional salt and serve.

> ⇨ *Pairs with* ⇦
> A protein dish (legumes,
> fish, or meat), a grain
> dish, and another
> vegetable or salad dish
> for a complete meal.

Shakshuka with Okra and Tomato

Okra is very rich in soluble fiber. It goes well with Middle Eastern spices, such as those used in shakshuka. Cooking them with something acidic, such as tomato or citrus, creates a nice texture. Generally, I try to cook with fresh or frozen vegetables rather than canned vegetables, but tomatoes are an exception. Fresh tomatoes are often refrigerated during transport to the supermarket, which makes them lose some of their flavor, so canned tomatoes are often more flavorful when tomatoes are out of season. Of course, if you have local tomatoes in season and they were harvested one or two days before, that is best. You can put eggs in this dish for a traditional shakshuka, or pair it with another protein dish if you don't want to include the eggs.

Preparation time: ①⓪ minutes
Cooking time: ②⑤ minutes
Serves ④
For vegan, omit the eggs

* ½ teaspoon cumin seeds
* ½ teaspoon coriander seeds
* ½ teaspoon mustard seeds
* ½ teaspoon ground sumac
* ½ teaspoon black peppercorns
* 2 tablespoons extra-virgin olive oil
* 1 medium onion, chopped
* 1 large green bell pepper, chopped
* 1 teaspoon chopped tarragon
* ½ teaspoon sea salt
* 1 lb (450 g) fresh tomatoes, diced, or 1 × 14.5 oz (400 g) can diced tomatoes
* 2 lb (900 g) okra, cut into 1-inch (2.5 cm) pieces
* Up to 4 eggs (1 per serving) (optional)
* 1 tablespoon chopped cilantro (coriander), for garnish

1. In a mortar and pestle (or spice grinder), combine the cumin seeds, coriander seeds, mustard seeds, sumac, and black peppercorns and grind to a powder.

2. In a large frying pan, heat the olive oil over medium heat. Add the onion and bell pepper and cook until fragrant and softened, about 3 minutes. Add the spice mix, tarragon, and salt and cook until fragrant, about 1 minute.

3. Add the tomatoes and okra, cover, and simmer until the okra is soft and tomato saucy, 15–20 minutes.

4. If using eggs, about 10 minutes into simmering, make the desired number of nests in the stew with a spoon. Crack one egg into each nest. Re-cover and simmer for 5–8 minutes, to your desired doneness of the eggs. Garnish with the cilantro (coriander).

> ⇥ *Pairs with* ⇤
> A protein dish (legumes, fish, or meat), a grain dish, and another vegetable or salad dish for a complete meal.

Vegetables and Tofu
with Herbs en Papillote

En papillote (*al cartoccio* in Italian, *pepes* in Indonesian, *zhibao* in Chinese) is a method of sealing food in a parchment paper packet and then baking it. The food is steamed by its own moisture, but unlike traditional steaming, the flavors are sealed inside the packet and don't evaporate during cooking, resulting in a flavorful dish as well as a healthy one. I've offered several choices of herbs to create different cultural flavors. Here, I use tofu as the protein, cooked together with a variety of vegetables, but this is also a good cooking method for tender fish fillets. The packet will puff up from the steam when cooked, and when opened on a plate just before eating, will release an explosion of rich aromas.

Preparation time: ②⓪ minutes
Cooking time: ①⑤ minutes
Serves ④
For nut-free, choose an appropriate seasoning option

* 1 lb (450 g) firm tofu, cut crosswise into 4 planks, each about 1 inch (2.5 cm) thick
* 4 small cauliflower florets
* 4 small broccoli or broccoli rabe (rapini) florets
* 4 white mushrooms, halved lengthwise through the stems
* 8 slices zucchini (courgette), ½ inch (1.25 cm) thick
* 8 slices yellow summer squash, ½ inch (1.25 cm) thick
* 8 slices orange carrot, ½ inch (1.25 cm) thick
* 8 slices purple carrot, ½ inch (1.25 cm) thick
* 8 green beans, trimmed
* 8 cloves garlic, unpeeled, tip and bottom of the cloves cut off
* Seasoning of choice (see *Seasoning options*)
* 1 tablespoon extra-virgin olive oil
* Pinch of salt

1. Preheat the oven to 400°F (200°C/ Gas Mark 6).
2. Cut four pieces of parchment paper into 12 × 16-inch (30 × 40 cm) rectangles. Fold each piece of parchment paper in half to make a 12 × 8-inch (30 × 20 cm) rectangle. Use kitchen shears to trim the folded parchment pieces into half-heart shapes.
3. Open up the parchment pieces and set them with the hearts' pointy-side facing you. Place a piece of tofu in the middle of the right half of each heart.
4. Dividing evenly, top the tofu with the vegetables, garlic, and seasoning of choice. Drizzle with the olive oil and season with the salt. Fold the left half of the heart over to enclose the ingredients. Seal the edge by making small overlapping folds, starting from the top and working your way down to the tip at the base. Fold the tip over to completely seal the packet.
5. Transfer the packets to a baking sheet. Bake until the vegetables are cooked through and crisp-tender, 8–12 minutes. The paper packets should puff up and turn slightly brownish.
6. Serve immediately. Transfer the packets to plates and let each diner open the packet carefully (there will be steam) for an explosion of colors and flavors.

Seasoning options

For a French flavor: 1 teaspoon dried herbes de Provence.

For an Italian flavor: ½ teaspoon finely chopped dried rosemary, ½ teaspoon finely chopped dried oregano, and 4 sweet basil leaves.

For an Eastern European flavor: 1 teaspoon finely chopped chives, 4 sprigs dill (each 2 inches/5 cm long), and a few mustard seeds.

For a Chinese flavor: 4 very thin slices fresh ginger and 1 tablespoon chopped scallion (spring onion).

For a Thai flavor: 4 lengths of lemongrass (each 1 inch/2.5 cm long), 4 Thai basil leaves, 4 very thin slices lime, and 1 Thai chili pepper (cut into four equal pieces).

Note: Nonvegetarians could also add a small piece of prosciutto or jamón Ibérico to each packet.

> → *Pairs with* ←
> A grain dish and another vegetable or salad dish for a complete meal.

Simmered Daikon Radish and Shiitake Mushrooms

Daikon radish (long white radish, icicle radish) is often eaten to "detox." Shiitake, along with kelp, add a savory umami taste to this mixture. The shiitake also contain polysaccharides which, when broken down by slow simmering, can help the immune system, while kelp is high in iodine, needed by the thyroid gland to function efficiently. This is a classic dish in Japanese cuisine—a vegan dish with numerous health benefits.

Preparation time: 10 minutes
Cooking time: 20 minutes
Serves 4

* 1–2 quarts (1–2 liters) hot water, plus extra boiling hot water if using dried mushrooms
* 4 oz (120 g) fresh or 2 oz (50 g) dried shiitake mushrooms
* 1 medium daikon radish, peeled and cut into rounds 1 inch (2.5 cm) thick
* 1 dried kelp square, about 4 × 4 inches (10 × 10 cm), broken into 1-inch (2.5 cm) squares
* 1 tablespoon gluten-free tamari
* 1 teaspoon mirin
* Fine sea salt
* Drizzle of sesame oil, for garnish
* 1 scallion (spring onion), green tops only, chopped, for garnish

1. If using dried shiitake mushrooms, in a heatproof bowl, soak in boiling hot water to cover for 10 minutes to rehydrate. Drain the mushrooms. Halve the rehydrated or fresh mushrooms lengthwise through the stems.

2. In a large saucepan, combine the mushrooms, daikon, kelp, tamari, mirin, and the hot water. Cover and bring to a boil, then reduce the heat, and simmer, covered, until the radishes are translucent and soft (a fork can go in easily), 15–20 minutes.

3. Season to taste with salt. Divide among four bowls. Top with a drizzle of sesame oil and scallion (spring onion) greens.

> → *Pairs with* ←
> A protein dish (legumes, fish, or meat), a grain dish, and another vegetable or salad dish for a complete meal.

Baby Bok Choy Braised with Oyster Sauce

Bok choy (or pak choi, which means "small white vegetable") is a leafy vegetable in the cabbage family. Each leaf has a thick and crunchy ivory stalk and a deep green leafy top. This combination gives it a unique mouthfeel. The stalk remains succulent when cooked and lends a meaty texture to the finished product. It has a mild taste and is rich in vitamins A, C, and K; it also contains quercetin, a substance that helps reduce inflammation in the body. Oyster sauce is a viscous dark brown sauce made from oyster extract and is rich and savory (find a version without MSG if you can). There are also vegetarian versions of "oyster sauce" made from mushroom extract instead of oysters.

Preparation time: ①⓪ minutes
Cooking time: ③⓪ minutes
Serves ④

* 2 tablespoons canola (rapeseed) oil
* 12 heads baby bok choy (fewer if each head is very large; more if very small), ¼ inch (6 mm) of the bottom end trimmed off, heads halved lengthwise
* 1 tablespoon oyster sauce
* ½ cup (4 fl oz/120 ml) water or stock
* 2 cloves garlic, crushed with the side of a knife and peeled
* Fine sea salt
* Freshly ground white pepper (optional)

1. In a large frying pan with a lid, heat the oil over medium heat until it becomes free-flowing. Working in batches of a few at a time, place the bok choy halves cut-side down in the pan to sear until lightly browned, 15–30 seconds.

2. When all the bok choy are seared, return them to the pan. Stir in the oyster sauce, water, garlic, ¼ teaspoon salt, and some white pepper (if using). Cover and simmer until the stalks are tender, 3–5 minutes.

3. Season to taste with salt. Remove the cooked bok choy and arrange side by side on a platter with the stalks on one end and leaves the other.

4. Bring the remaining sauce in the pan to a boil and simmer until thickened. Pour over the bok choy and serve.

> → *Pairs with* ←
> A protein dish (legumes, fish, or meat), a grain dish, and another vegetable or salad dish for a complete meal.

Roasted Butternut Squash Soup

Butternut squash is rich in vitamin A. It can be boiled, sautéed, or roasted, and it also makes a great silky and creamy soup. Some recipes use boiled squash to make soup, but I like to roast it in its skin to develop a smoky, nutty flavor and to preserve its moisture. The herbs add complexity to the flavors and the pine nuts enhance the nuttiness of the squash.

Preparation time: 10 minutes
Cooking time: 1 hour 10 minutes
Serves 4

* 1 butternut squash (about 2 lb/ 900 g), halved lengthwise, seeds removed
* 1 teaspoon chopped rosemary
* 1 teaspoon chopped thyme
* ¼ teaspoon plus a pinch of coarse sea salt
* 1 tablespoon extra-virgin olive oil
* 1 teaspoon pine nuts
* 3-4 cups (25-32 fl oz/750-950 ml) hot water
* 1 teaspoon finely chopped chives, for garnish
* A few dill sprigs, for garnish

1. Preheat the oven to 350°F (180°C/Gas Mark 4).

2. Place the squash cut-side up on a baking sheet. Sprinkle with the rosemary, thyme, and a pinch of salt. Drizzle with the olive oil.

3. Transfer to the oven and roast until the flesh is soft all the way through, about 1 hour. Add the pine nuts to the baking sheet to toast in the last 10 minutes.

4. Lightly scrape off any herbs on the surface of the squash using a spoon. (Or leave them on if you prefer the soup to have stronger flavors.) Scoop the flesh of the squash into a 2-quart (64 fl oz/ 1.8-liter) pot or saucepan and add 3 cups (25 fl oz/750 ml) of the hot water. Purée with a hand blender. If the soup is too thick, blend in up to 1 cup (8 fl oz/250 ml) additional water, a little at a time, to reach your desired consistency.

5. Add the remaining ¼ teaspoon salt, bring to a boil over low heat, and simmer until heated through and smooth. Transfer to bowls and garnish with the chives, dill sprigs, and toasted pine nuts.

> → *Pairs with* ←
> A protein dish (legumes, fish, or meat), a grain dish, and another vegetable or salad dish for a complete meal.

Legumes

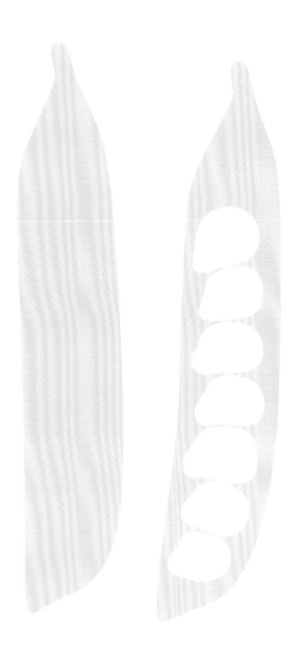

Lentil Dal

Dal is a staple in Indian cuisine, made from several kinds of legume, lentils being the most common—the masoor dal. It can also be made from pigeon peas (toor dal), chickpeas (chana dal), or urad beans (urad dal)—all of which are high in plant protein. Some recipes use preboiled lentils, but I like to fry the lentils with spices first and then add the boiling water. The frying starts a Maillard reaction (page 19) and creates more complex and savory flavors. Adding hot water helps preserve the substances that give the umami taste.

Preparation time: ⑤ minutes
Cooking time: ②⑤ minutes
Serves ④

* ¼ teaspoon each fenugreek seeds, coriander seeds, mustard seeds, caraway seeds, fennel seeds, and black peppercorns (see *Note*)
* 1 green cardamom pod
* 2 cloves garlic, minced
* 2 tablespoons extra-virgin olive oil
* 1 tablespoon ghee
* ½ medium red onion, chopped
* 1 small tomato, chopped
* 2 teaspoons ground turmeric
* ½ teaspoon coarse sea salt
* 2 cups (400 g) split yellow, red, or green lentils, rinsed
* 1 tablespoon chopped cilantro (coriander)

1. In a small saucepan, bring 4 cups (32 fl oz/950 ml) water to a simmer.

2. In a mortar and pestle (or spice grinder), crush and then grind the seed spices, cardamom pod, and garlic into a fine paste.

3. In a medium saucepan, heat the olive oil and ghee over medium heat. Add the spice paste and fry until fragrant, 15–30 seconds. Add the onion and tomato and cook until fragrant, 1–2 minutes.

4. Add the turmeric and salt and stir until well combined, about 1 minute. Add the lentils and mix thoroughly. Let cook undisturbed for 1 minute to get the Maillard reaction going. Stir to mix, then cook for 1 more minute undisturbed.

5. Add the hot water slowly, being careful not to splash. Cover the pan, reduce the heat to low, and simmer until the lentils start to break up, about 20 minutes, stirring occasionally. Add more hot water, as needed, to achieve your desired consistency.

6. Transfer to bowls and sprinkle with the cilantro (coriander).

Note: When cooking, use whole spice seeds whenever possible and grind them in a mortar and pestle right before cooking to really bring your dishes alive. The fragrance from the spice starts to evaporate as soon as it is ground. Bottled spices are convenient but have already lost some of their flavor.

⟶ *Pairs with* ⟵
A grain dish and ②
vegetable or salad dishes
for a complete meal.

Lima Bean Chili
with Green Beans

This is a vegan dish rich in protein. Lima beans (butter beans) are high in fiber, which cultivates a healthy gut microbiome, while the other beans add complexity of flavor. Use dried beans when you can, as they taste so much better and have more nutritional value than canned beans. If you would like to add some meat to the chili, add about 8 ounces (225 grams) ground (minced) turkey or beef when sautéing the onion. Because this dish takes a long time to make, you can double or triple the recipe for the freezer. Cook until you add the green beans or collards, then freeze or refrigerate and add the green vegetables when you reheat, simmering for 10 minutes.

Preparation time: 15 minutes,
plus overnight soaking
Cooking time: 1 hour 20 minutes
Serves 4

* 4 oz (120 g) dried lima beans
  (butter beans)
* 4 oz (120 g) other dried beans,
  such as red kidney, navy (haricot),
  or black beans
* 1 teaspoon cumin seeds
* ½ teaspoon fennel seeds
* ½ teaspoon black peppercorns
* ½ teaspoon cayenne pepper
* ½ teaspoon sweet paprika
* 1 allspice berry
* 1 whole clove
* 2 tablespoons olive oil
* ½ medium onion, chopped
* 4 cloves garlic, minced
* 1 stalk celery, chopped
* 1 lb (450 g) tomatoes (any kind),
  chopped
* 3 small dried Mexican puya
  (pulla) or guajillo chilies, coarsely
  chopped, with seeds
* 2–3 cups (16–25 fl oz/475–750 ml)
  water or vegetable stock, as needed
* 12 oz (350 g) green beans, trimmed,
  or chopped collard greens
* Coarse sea salt
* 1 small bunch cilantro (coriander),
  chopped (optional)

1. Soak all the dried beans in water to cover for 8 hours or overnight, depending on your own cooking schedule. Drain and rinse well.

2. In a large pot, combine the beans with water to cover by 2 inches (5 cm). Bring to a boil, then reduce the heat to a simmer and parcook until almost tender, about 30 minutes. Drain.

3. In a mortar and pestle (or spice grinder), combine the cumin seeds, fennel seeds, peppercorns, cayenne, paprika, allspice, and clove and grind.

4. In a Dutch oven (casserole) or large pot, heat the olive oil over medium heat. Add the onion, garlic, and celery and cook until slightly softened, about 2 minutes. Stir in the spice mixture and cook until fragrant, about 2 minutes. Add the tomatoes and chilies. Cook, stirring occasionally, until the tomatoes soften and break down, about 2 minutes.

5. Add 2 cups (16 fl oz/475 ml) water or stock and bring to a boil. Add the parcooked beans and enough of the remaining water or stock so the beans are covered. Simmer until the chili is thickened and the beans are tender, about 30 minutes.

6. Add the green beans, cover, and simmer until tender, about 10 minutes. Season to taste with salt. Sprinkle with the cilantro (coriander), if desired, and serve.

> → *Pairs with* ←
> A grain dish and 2
> vegetable or salad dishes
> for a complete meal.

Fava Beans with Porcini Mushrooms and Sun-Dried Tomatoes

Fava beans (broad beans) contain an ideal ratio of macronutrients: 25 percent protein, 25 percent fiber, 35 percent starch, and 10 percent water. They have a more savory taste than other beans and are often underutilized in our diet. I add porcini mushrooms and sun-dried tomatoes to boost both flavor and nutritional complexity.

Preparation time: ⑤ minutes, plus ③⓪ minutes' soaking time if using dried mushrooms
Cooking time: ②⓪ minutes
Serves ④

* 4 fresh porcini mushrooms, thinly sliced, or ¼ cup (10 g) dried porcini mushroom slices
* 2 lb (900 g) fresh or frozen peeled fava beans (broad beans)
* 2 tablespoons olive oil
* 4 cloves garlic, peeled and crushed
* ¼ cup (40 g) sun-dried tomatoes, either dry-packed or drained oil-packed
* ½ teaspoon coarse sea salt

1. If using dried porcini, soak them in 1 cup (8 fl oz/250 ml) water for 30 minutes to rehydrate. When ready to use, drain but reserve the soaking water.

2. Bring a large pot of unsalted water to a boil. Add the fava beans (broad beans) and blanch for 1 minute. Drain without cooling and set aside.

3. In a large frying pan, heat the olive oil over medium heat. Add the garlic and sauté until fragrant, about 2 minutes. Add the sun-dried tomatoes and cook until penetrated by the oil, about 1 minute. Add the sliced fresh or rehydrated mushrooms and cook uncovered until browned, about 2 minutes.

4. Add the fava beans. (If using rehydrated mushrooms, add their soaking water here. If you're using fresh mushrooms, they will have released juices when they cooked.) Stir and cook, covered, over medium-low heat until cooked through, 8–10 minutes. Uncover and adjust the heat so the sauce reduces to coat the beans. Season with the salt.

> → *Pairs with* ←
> A grain dish and ② vegetable or salad dishes for a complete meal.

Chickpeas with Farro, Parsley, Cucumber, and Tomato

Chickpeas are nutrient-dense and high in plant protein, and they can be a good substitute for animal protein. Farro, a sister species to common wheat, is a whole grain that has a chewy and nutty quality when cooked. When combined with vegetables, you'll have a dish comprehensive in nutrients. When cooking chickpeas, adding some spices will infuse them with flavor, while the apple brings sweetness, to balance the sharpness of the parsley and onions.

Preparation time: 10 minutes, plus overnight soaking if using dried chickpeas
Cooking time: 1 hour 30 minutes (40 minutes if using canned chickpeas)
Serves 4

* 1½ cups (300 g) dried chickpeas (also known as garbanzo beans or chana) or 2 cans (10 oz/280 g each) chickpeas, drained and rinsed
* 1 bay leaf (if using dried chickpeas)
* 1 allspice berry (if using dried chickpeas)
* 1 cup (200 g) farro
* 2 cups (120 g) finely chopped parsley
* 6 plum tomatoes, diced
* 2 medium cucumbers, peeled and cut into 1-inch (2.5 cm) chunks
* 1 medium white sweet onion, diced
* 2 apples, unpeeled and diced
* 3 tablespoons extra-virgin olive oil
* 1 tablespoon fresh lemon juice
* 1 teaspoon ground cumin
* ½ teaspoon coarse sea salt
* Pinch of freshly ground black pepper

1. If using dried chickpeas, soak them in water to cover by several inches (at least 8 cm) overnight.

2. Drain the chickpeas and transfer to a saucepan. Add the bay leaf, allspice, and water to cover by 2 inches (5 cm). Bring to a boil, then reduce the heat and simmer, covered, until cooked through but not crumbly, 1 hour to 1 hour 30 minutes. Drain and rinse with cold water. (Skip this step if using canned beans.)

3. Meanwhile, rinse the farro and drain. Transfer to a medium saucepan and add water to cover by 2 inches (5 cm). Bring to a boil, then reduce the heat to a simmer, cover, and cook until cooked through but still chewy and not mushy, 20–40 minutes, depending on the brand of farro. Drain and rinse with cold water.

4. In a large bowl, combine the cooked dried or canned chickpeas, farro, parsley, tomatoes, cucumbers, onion, and apples. Drizzle with the olive oil and lemon juice, and season with the cumin, salt, and pepper. Toss evenly to combine.

> → *Pairs with* ←
> A grain dish and a
> vegetable or salad dish for
> a complete meal.

Kimchi Tofu Stew

Kimchi is napa cabbage (Chinese leaf) and radish pickled with garlic, onion, and chili pepper. As a result, it is quite pungent and spicy. Tofu can be relatively bland and is able to absorb flavor from other ingredients when cooked together, so it pairs well with kimchi in this hearty stew. Raw kimchi is full of probiotics and intense flavors. The most savory and tasty kimchi usually has anchovy or other seafood mixed in before fermentation starts. Look for "anchovy" or "shrimp" in the ingredient list, unless you're vegetarian or vegan. This is a typical Korean dish, and it warms the stomach, so is best on a cold wintry day.

Preparation time: ①⓪ minutes
Cooking time: ①⑤ minutes
Serves ④
For vegan/vegetarian, omit the dried shrimp and ensure the kimchi is vegan-friendly; for vegan, also omit the eggs

* 2 tablespoons canola (rapeseed) oil
* 2 cloves garlic, sliced
* 1–2 tablespoons gochujang (depending on your preference for heat)
* 1 cup (5 oz/150 g) kimchi
* 2 boxes (16 oz/450 g each) soft tofu, drained and cut into 1-inch (2.5 cm) cubes
* 1 scallion (spring onion), finely chopped
* 1 teaspoon dried shrimp (optional)
* 4 eggs (optional)

1. In a large saucepan, heat the oil over medium heat. Add the garlic and cook until fragrant, about 1 minute. Add the gochujang and cook until fragrant, about 1 minute. Add the kimchi, stir, and cook until softened, about 2 minutes.

2. Add 4 cups (32 fl oz/950 ml) water and the tofu. Simmer over medium-low heat, uncovered, for 5 minutes to let the flavor from the soup penetrate the tofu somewhat. (No salt is needed since the kimchi is quite salty.)

3. Transfer to four medium bowls. Sprinkle with the scallion (spring onion) and dried shrimp (if using). If you'd like, crack 1 egg into each bowl of stew. Let the heat from the stew cook the egg slightly, so the edge is set but the center is still runny, about 5 minutes.

Note: If you use live-culture kimchi (not pasteurized), you can add a little of the kimchi fluid to the stew after it has cooled down to about room temperature. It is full of probiotics that help our microbiota.

> → *Pairs with* ←
> A grain dish and ②
> vegetable or salad dishes
> for a complete meal.

Vegan Tempeh Burger

Tempeh is a firm soybean cake that has gone through a special fermentation process. Because soybeans are very rich in plant protein, the fermentation generates a savory taste, and the consistency is like a meat patty or grilled chicken, which means tempeh can be used to make a tasty vegan burger. Whole soybeans are used to make tempeh, whereas tofu, another plant-protein-rich soy product, is made of soybean extract. This gives tempeh a more complex nutrient profile than tofu, with more fiber and micronutrients. The fermentation process also breaks down protein, fat, and fibers, making tempeh easy to digest. In addition to burgers, tempeh can be used in many other vegan dishes: It's a great substitute for grilled chicken in a salad, and is also delicious and holds its shape in a stew or rich sauce.

Preparation time: 10 minutes, plus marinating time
Cooking time: 30 minutes
Serves 4

* 2 packets (8 oz/225 g each) tempeh, each cut crosswise to create 4 square patties
* 1 tablespoon vegan barbecue sauce
* 1 teaspoon balsamic vinegar
* 1 teaspoon sugar
* 1 onion, ¼ chopped and ¾ sliced into rings
* 2 tablespoons canola (rapeseed) oil
* 4 whole-wheat or seeded hamburger buns, split
* 1 Hass avocado, sliced
* 1 beefsteak tomato, sliced
* 4 lettuce leaves
* Fine sea salt and freshly ground black pepper

1. Prepare a steamer fitted with a rack (see *Note*). Arrange the tempeh on the rack and steam, covered, for 15 minutes to cook through. (This cooks the tempeh and also removes the residual bitter taste from the fermentation.)

2. Remove the steamed tempeh patties and pat dry. Place in a wide, shallow bowl. Add the barbecue sauce, vinegar, sugar, chopped onion, and 1 tablespoon of the oil and let marinate for 15 minutes.

3. While marinating, toast the buns and prepare the vegetables.

4. Heat a large frying pan that can fit all four patties at once over medium heat. When hot, add the remaining 1 tablespoon oil and the onion rings. Cook over low heat until caramelized, 3–5 minutes. Remove and set aside.

5. Increase the heat to medium. Add the tempeh patties. Cook until fragrant and browned on one side, 1–2 minutes. Flip and cook the other side in the same manner. Season the tempeh and onions to taste with salt and pepper.

6. Assemble the burgers, starting with the tempeh patties, followed by the avocado, tomato, lettuce, and onion.

Note: If you don't have a steamer, bring 2 inches (5 cm) of water to a simmer in a large pot. Put the tempeh in a heatproof bowl that will fit in the pot without touching the sides. Steam, covered, over medium heat, for 15 minutes.

> → *Pairs with* ←
> Any salad dish for a
> complete meal.

Cannellini Bean Soup

This hearty soup is inspired by Galician hot soup (caldo gallego) and Tuscan bean soup. It is rich in protein from the beans and fiber from the vegetables. Use dried beans, although canned beans are fine if you are in a hurry. You can substitute other white beans, such as navy (haricot) or Great Northern beans. This can serve as a stand-alone light supper, or a lunch with a piece of crusty bread. Chorizo is here mainly for flavor; you can remove it at the end if you don't like the texture, as the flavors will have already been blended into the soup during the long cooking process.

Preparation time: 20 minutes, plus 1–8 hours' soaking time if using dried beans
Cooking time: 50 minutes (20 minutes if using canned beans)
Serves 4

* 1 cup (200 g) dried white kidney (cannellini) beans or 1 can (15 oz/ 425 g) cannellini, drained and rinsed
* 2 tablespoons extra-virgin olive oil
* 1 medium onion, chopped
* 1 large carrot, chopped
* 3 stalks celery, chopped
* 4 cloves garlic, minced
* ½ teaspoon dried oregano or 1 teaspoon chopped fresh
* ½ teaspoon dried thyme or 1 teaspoon chopped fresh
* 1 bay leaf
* 4 oz (120 g) cured Spanish chorizo, cut into ½-inch (1.25 cm) chunks
* 2 tablespoons sherry
* 1 teaspoon tomato paste (tomato purée)
* 10 cups (80 fl oz/2.4 liters) hot water
* 1 medium russet (baking) potato, peeled and chopped
* 2 cups (200 g) packed chopped greens (turnip greens, collard greens, Swiss chard, kale, or bok choy)
* Kosher (flaked) salt

1. Soak the dried beans, if using, for 1 hour in warm water or overnight in cool water, depending on how it fits your cooking schedule. Drain.

2. Heat a large pot over medium heat and add the olive oil. Add the onion, carrot, celery, garlic, and herbs and cook until fragrant, 2–3 minutes. Add the chorizo, sherry, and tomato paste (purée). Cook until the tomato paste thickens, about 2 minutes.

3. Add the hot water, potato, and cooked dried or canned beans. Cover and simmer over medium-low heat until the beans are broken down and tender, and the soup is thickened, about 40 minutes (10–15 minutes if using canned beans).

4. Stir vigorously to further break down the beans. Add the greens. Simmer, covered, until the greens are tender, about 10 minutes. Season to taste with salt.

> → *Pairs with* ←
> A protein dish, a grain dish, and a vegetable or salad dish for a complete meal. It can also serve as a light meal on its own.

Green Pea Purée with Tomatoes and Cauliflower

Green peas are a very versatile ingredient. They are most commonly just boiled and served as a "vegetable" side dish, but because they are actually the young seeds of the pea plant, they have a higher amount of protein than the average vegetable and can serve as a main player in a light meal. Combined with a fruit (tomato), a flower (cauliflower), and another seed (pecan), this makes a very balanced vegan dish that contains all of the macronutrients.

Preparation time: ⑤ minutes
Cooking time: ①⑤ minutes
Serves ④

* ½ medium head cauliflower, cored and broken into 2-inch (5 cm) florets
* 3¾ cups (450 g) frozen green peas
* 2 tablespoons extra-virgin olive oil
* 1–2 cups (8–16 fl oz/250–475 ml) water or vegetable stock
* 16 cherry tomatoes, halved crosswise
* ½ cup (60 g) pecans, toasted
* Coarse sea salt and freshly ground black pepper

1. In a large pot of boiling water (at least 4 quarts/liters), cook the cauliflower until crisp-tender, 3–5 minutes. Scoop out the cauliflower and transfer to a bowl or pot of cold water under a running tap to stop the cooking. Drain and set aside.

2. Bring the pot of water to a rolling boil again. Add the peas and cook until bright green, 1–2 minutes. Drain the peas in a colander under cold running water to stop the cooking. Remove when the peas are warm to touch.

3. In a blender, combine the peas, ¼ teaspoon salt, the olive oil, and 1 cup (8 fl oz/250 ml) water and blend at medium speed. Gradually add up to 1 more cup (8 fl oz/250 ml) water, a little at a time, to reach a consistency you like. (I like it to be slightly thinner than mashed potato.)

4. Divide the purée among four bowls. Top with the tomatoes, cauliflower, and pecans. Season with salt and pepper to taste.

Variation: You can also mash the peas, omitting the water or stock. Combine the peas, salt, and oil and mash to a coarse consistency. The mashed peas can be formed into four cakes ½–1-inch (1.25–2.5 cm) thick and pan-fried to brown them a little. Serve topped with the tomato, cauliflower, salt, and pepper.

→ *Pairs with* ←
A small amount of protein, such as some dal, plus a small amount of carbohydrate, such as a whole-grain dinner roll for a complete meal. It can also serve as a light meal on its own.

Edamame with Roasted Cauliflower Steaks

Edamame are immature green soybeans in their pod. Because the beans are still young, they are more tender and sweet. They're packed with a nutritional punch, and have more amino acids than mature beans. We see them most often served in Japanese restaurants as a small appetizer or side dish, but here they are an equal partner to roasted cauliflower steaks. (You can also use shelled edamame in this dish instead of the pods.) Cooking with fresh edamame is best, but they don't last longer than one or two days before losing flavor—luckily, frozen edamame are now widely available and a good substitute. Frozen edamame also make a good snack, much healthier than potato chips or pretzels. They usually come cooked, salted, and frozen; simply soak in boiling hot water for a few minutes or microwave for 1 to 2 minutes.

Preparation time: ①⓪ minutes
Cooking time: ③⓪ minutes
Serves ④

* 1 large head cauliflower (about 2 lb/900 g), trimmed of leaves
* 2 tablespoons avocado oil
* 2 cloves garlic, minced
* 1 teaspoon finely chopped fresh rosemary
* 1 teaspoon sweet paprika
* ½ teaspoon fine sea salt
* 3 cups (450 g) frozen edamame pods (usually precooked), thawed

1. Preheat the oven to 450°F (230°C/Gas Mark 8).

2. Halve the cauliflower head through the stem. Cut parallel to the center to make four ½-inch (1.25 cm) thick steaks. Set aside the remaining small loose florets that have crumbled off.

3. Set the cauliflower steaks on a baking sheet and brush both sides with the oil. Sprinkle both sides with the garlic, rosemary, paprika, and salt.

4. Roast for 15 minutes, flip and continue to roast until the other side is browned and cooked through, 10–15 minutes more.

5. Meanwhile, bring a pot of water to boil. Remove from the heat, add the thawed edamame and soak for 1 minute if you like crunchy beans, or up to 5 minutes if you like soft beans. Drain and pat dry.

6. Transfer the cauliflower steaks to plates and sprinkle with the remaining uncooked florets. Serve the edamame pods on the side (or on top if using shelled beans). Eat the edamame by picking up a pod by the stem end, putting the whole pod in the mouth and squeezing the beans out of the pod with your teeth while pulling the pod from the mouth. Discard the pod.

> ⇾ *Pairs with* ⇽
> A protein dish, such as a fish dish, and a small bowl of brown rice for a complete meal.

Fish, Shellfish, Poultry & Meats

Tuna Steak with Cucumber and Carrot Ribbons

Tuna is full of protein and high in omega-3 fatty acids. It has a neutral flavor so can be enjoyed by those who aren't keen on fish. Use the freshest tuna you can find, preferably sashimi grade. Flash-seared, this dish combines the flavors of cooked and raw fish. The substantive protein from tuna is paired with crunchy fresh vegetables. Here, I add no salt other than that used to marinate the tuna, to highlight the vegetables' refreshing flavors.

Preparation time: 20 minutes
Cooking time: 5 minutes
Serves 4

* 1 teaspoon grated fresh ginger
* 1 teaspoon toasted sesame oil
* ½ teaspoon sweet paprika
* ¼ teaspoon kosher (flaked) salt
* 2 very fresh tuna steaks (6–8 oz/ 175–225 g each), 1 inch (2.5 cm) thick
* 2 slicing cucumbers or 1 English (seedless) cucumber
* 2 large carrots
* 2 small zucchini (courgettes)
* 2 teaspoons balsamic vinegar
* 2 tablespoons avocado oil
* Splash of white wine
* Pinch of freshly ground black pepper
* Toasted sesame seeds or chopped toasted nuts (optional), for garnish

1. In a small bowl, mix the ginger, sesame oil, paprika, and salt. Rub the mixture onto the tuna steaks on a plate and marinate for 15 minutes.

2. While the tuna marinates, prepare vegetable ribbons by using a vegetable peeler to pull off lengthwise ribbons from the cucumbers, carrots, and zucchini (courgettes), discarding the seed/core portions. Roll the ribbons (a few at a time if you want to do it quickly, or individually if you have time to make them look pretty) and arrange on four plates. Drizzle with the balsamic vinegar.

3. In a well-seasoned cast-iron skillet, heat the avocado oil over high heat until it ripples. Place the tuna steaks (reserving the plate they were on) in the pan. Watch the sides of the steak and cook until the bottom ⅛ inch (3 mm) turns opaque, about 30 seconds. Flip to sear the other side in the same manner. Remove the pan from the heat and set the tuna aside.

4. Add the splash of white wine to the tuna plate to dissolve any remaining seasonings and pour into the pan, stirring to mix with the juices in the pan.

5. Thinly slice the tuna with a very sharp knife. Lay on top of the vegetable ribbons. Drizzle the pan juices on top of the tuna and sprinkle with the black pepper. If desired, garnish with sesame seeds or chopped nuts.

> ⇢ *Pairs with* ⇠
> A grain dish and a
> vegetable or salad dish for
> a complete meal.

Baked Salmon and Tomato with Blanched Kale

Salmon plus tomato plus kale creates a dish of healthy ingredients and brilliant colors. Salmon is an oily fish, rich in omega-3 fatty acids, so when cooking salmon I use less oil than for other fish. Salmon has a thicker and tougher skin than other fish fillets. Cook it skin-side down so that the skin becomes softened. Or, if you enjoy crunchy skin, before removing the salmon from the oven, broil (grill) the skin for 1–2 minutes to crisp it up. The time it takes to cook the fish depends on its thickness and fat content. In general, when a fork can easily separate the fish into flakes, it is done.

Preparation time: ⑤ minutes
Cooking time: ①⑤ minutes
Serves ②

* 2 tablespoons extra-virgin olive oil
* 1 large tomato, sliced crosswise into 4 thick slices
* 12 oz (350 g) skin-on salmon fillet
* 1 teaspoon distilled white vinegar or 1 wedge of lemon
* ½ teaspoon coarse sea salt
* ¼ teaspoon freshly ground black pepper
* 1 teaspoon chopped tarragon or ½ teaspoon dried
* 10 oz (280 g) kale, tough stems trimmed, leaves roughly torn

1. Preheat the oven to 425°F (220°C/Gas Mark 7).

2. Bring a large pot of water to a boil for blanching the kale. Put a large sieve or colander in the sink.

3. Brush a sheet pan with 1½ tablespoons of the olive oil. Turn the tomato slices to coat in the olive oil and set on one side of the sheet pan. Place the salmon fillet skin-side down on the other side of the pan. Drizzle the vinegar (or squeeze the lemon juice) evenly on top of the fillet and sprinkle with ¼ teaspoon of the salt, the pepper, and tarragon. Let marinate for 5 minutes.

4. Transfer the salmon to the oven (if you like crispy skin, flip the fillet so that the skin side is up before putting the pan in the oven). Roast the salmon until just cooked through, 12–15 minutes.

5. Meanwhile, add the kale to the boiling water all at once, stirring immediately. Once the water returns to a boil, after 15 seconds, tip the kale into the sieve. Rinse with copious amounts of cool running water so the temperature of the kale drops to room temperature as quickly as possible. Press as much water as possible from the kale pieces until they are dry.

6. Transfer the kale to a medium bowl. Sprinkle with the remaining ¼ teaspoon salt and ½ tablespoon olive oil and toss.

7. Make a bed of kale on each of two large plates. Cut the salmon fillet into serving pieces and transfer to the plates along with the tomato slices. Pour the juices left on the sheet pan over the salmon pieces.

→ *Pairs with* ←
A grain dish and a vegetable or salad dish for a complete meal.

Miso-Baked White Fish

Miso—fermented soybean paste—is a nutritious vegan seasoning. During fermentation, the enzymes break down the proteins and carbohydrates in soybeans and produce umami-tasting by-products. Miso can replace sauce or seasoning made of meat stock or dairy products (butter or cheese) without losing the flavor-enhancing effect. Shio koji is a fermented rice paste containing a different set of umami-producing compounds and a little bit of alcohol, which brings out even more flavor from the fish. Any mild-flavored white fish, such as sea bass, cod, haddock, or snapper, would work well for this dish.

Preparation time: ⑤ minutes, plus overnight marinating time
Cooking time: ②⓪ minutes
Serves ④
For gluten-free, use dashi

* 2 tablespoons white miso
* 1 tablespoon shio koji (fermented rice paste) or 1 more tablespoon miso
* 1 tablespoon mild-flavored vegetable oil, such as canola (rapeseed) oil
* 1 tablespoon sugar
* 3 tablespoons rice wine
* ½ tablespoon rice vinegar
* 4 skinless white fish fillets (such as cod, haddock, snapper or sea bass), about 6 oz/175 g each and 1 inch/2.5 cm thick
* 2 tablespoons finely chopped scallions (spring onions)
* Mushroom sauce (shop-bought) or Dashi (page 68) (optional)

1. In a glass or ceramic baking dish large enough to hold the fish in one layer, combine the miso, shio koji, oil, sugar, wine, and vinegar. Mix to form a smooth paste.

2. Dry the fish with paper towels. Add the fillets to the marinade in the baking dish and turn to coat them. Cover and refrigerate for at least 8 or up to 16 hours, depending on your schedule.

3. When you're ready to cook, preheat the oven to 350°F (180°C/Gas Mark 4).

4. Use a spoon to gently scrape off most of the marinade from the fish, leaving just a very thin layer. Discard the marinade and wipe the baking dish clean, then return the fish to the dish.

5. Bake the fish until it starts to flake, about 20 minutes, depending on thickness.

6. Increase the oven temperature to 450°F (230°C/Gas Mark 8) and roast until the fish develops a golden crust, about 5 minutes. (You could also broil/grill the fish at this point.)

7. Sprinkle with the scallions (spring onions) and drizzle with mushroom sauce or dashi, if using.

> → *Pairs with* ←
> A grain dish and ② vegetable or salad dishes for a complete meal.

Soy Sauce-Braised Pompano

With its reddish, firm flesh and unique sweet and nutty taste, pompano is highly prized. If you get "fresh-out-of-the-water" pompano, you can also steam it: See Steamed Whole Branzino with Scallions and Ginger (page 181) or Vegetables and Tofu with Herbs en Papillote (page 135) for detailed instructions. Here I use wine, soy sauce, and vinegar to braise it for a richly flavored, healthy protein dish.

Preparation time: ①⓪ minutes
Cooking time: ①⓪ minutes
Serves ④
For gluten-free, use gluten-free tamari

* 2 skin-on pompano fillets (about 8 oz/225 g each), halved crosswise
* 2 teaspoons cornstarch (cornflour)
* ¼ cup (2 fl oz/60 ml) olive oil
* 1 scallion (spring onion), cut into 1-inch (2.5 cm) lengths
* 1-inch piece (15 g) fresh ginger, sliced
* ½ cup (4 fl oz/120 ml) rice wine or white wine
* ½ cup (4 fl oz/120 ml) hot water
* 2 teaspoons rice vinegar or white wine vinegar
* 2 teaspoons soy sauce or gluten-free tamari
* 2 teaspoons sugar
* 1 teaspoon drained brine-packed capers
* 1 orange wedge (about ¼ orange)
* 1 tablespoon microgreens (optional), for garnish
* Kosher (flaked) salt

1. Dust each fish fillet on both sides with a thin coating of cornstarch (cornflour).

2. In a large frying pan, heat the oil over medium heat. Lay the fillets in the pan flesh-side down. Reduce the heat to medium-low and cook undisturbed until the fillets move freely without sticking to the pan, about 4 minutes.

3. Flip and repeat, pressing down on the fillets so they make full contact with the base of the pan.

4. Add the scallion (spring onion) and ginger slices in the open spaces in the pan. Add the wine, water, vinegar, soy sauce, sugar, and capers. Squeeze the orange wedge into the pan. Mix in the juice and use the liquid to baste the fillets. Cover and simmer until cooked through, about 3 minutes.

5. Plate the fillets with the skin side down. If desired, sprinkle the microgreens on top.

6. Simmer the pan juices over medium heat until thickened, season with salt if needed, and pour over the top.

> → *Pairs with* ←
> A grain dish and ②
> vegetable or salad dishes
> for a complete meal.

Pan-Fried Flounder Fillet with Onion and Parsley

Flounder is very tender and subtle in taste. Even people who don't like fish might enjoy this delicately flavored dish. When pan-frying fish fillets, make sure the fillet is patted very dry and evenly coated with the starch. This makes the fish crisp on the outside and moist inside. If the surface of the fish is not super dry, the starch won't stick and the moisture in the fish could leak out and ruin the dish. I use cornstarch (cornflour) here because it's fine-textured and adheres more evenly to the little crevices in the fish, giving a thinner coating without sacrificing the sealing effect. I use my hand to rub the starch into the fillet, rather than coating it by dusting or rolling. The pressure makes the starch stick to the flesh, so the coating won't come off during pan-frying.

Preparation time: ①◎ minutes
Cooking time: ①⑤ minutes
Serves ②

* 2 flounder fillets (about 6 oz/175 g each)
* ½ teaspoon kosher (flaked) salt
* Cornstarch (cornflour), for dusting
* 2 tablespoons olive oil
* ½ tablespoon (7 g) unsalted butter
* ½ medium red onion, chopped
* ½ cup (15 g) chopped parsley leaves
* 3 tablespoons mirin (or 3 tablespoons white wine mixed with 2 teaspoons sugar)
* 2 tablespoons apple cider vinegar
* Lemon wedges for serving (optional)

1. Pat the fillets very dry with paper towels. Sprinkle evenly on both sides with the salt. Lay them on two layers of paper towel. Cover with another two layers and apply pressure so that the paper towels make full contact with the entire fillet. Let sit for 5 minutes to make sure the fillets are as dry as possible.

2. Remove the paper towels and rub the fish evenly on both sides with a thin layer of cornstarch (cornflour).

3. In a well-seasoned cast-iron skillet, heat the olive oil over high heat until hot but not smoking. Lay the fillets flat-side down (the side where the skin was) so they don't curl up when cooked. Reduce the heat to medium and cook until the underside is golden and the fillet no longer sticks to the bottom of the pan, about 3 minutes. Flip the fillets and cook until the second side is golden, 2–3 minutes more, pressing the edges down occasionally so the entire side is in contact with the pan. Transfer to a platter or serving plates.

4. Add the butter to the pan and when melted, add the onion and stir. Cook until the onion softens and is fragrant, about 3 minutes. Add the parsley, stir, and immediately add the mirin and vinegar. Stir to combine into a sauce and remove from the heat. Pour the sauce over the fish and serve with lemon wedges alongside, if desired.

> → *Pairs with* ←
> A grain dish and ② vegetable or salad dishes for a complete meal.

Pan-Seared Sea Bass

Sea bass has flaky white flesh with a mild and slightly sweet taste and is a healthy marine protein. I especially like black sea bass for its texture and flavor. Because of its delicate flavor, it is best cooked with minimal seasonings—here, I use only salt on the fish before cooking. Avocado oil has a high smoke point so can be heated to a higher cooking temperature for crispier skin. Leeks are fragrant but milder than onion or garlic with a bit of a sweet taste and pair well with the sea bass. When served on top of a bed of mild baby greens, with no dressing other than the juice from the fish and leek, this is a healthy and delicious dish.

Preparation time: ⑤ minutes
Cooking time: ①⓪ minutes
Serves ④

* 2 skin-on sea bass fillets (6–8 oz/175–225 g each), halved crosswise
* ¼ teaspoon plus a pinch of coarse sea salt
* 3 tablespoons avocado oil
* 1 leek, white and light-green parts only, halved lengthwise and finely sliced
* 2 tablespoons dry white wine
* 5 oz (150 g) baby greens, such as kale, spinach, or arugula (rocket)
* Juice of ¼ lemon, plus wedges for serving (optional)
* Pinch of freshly ground black or white pepper

1. Pat the fish fillets dry. Sprinkle ¼ teaspoon of the salt all over and rub it in.

2. In a large frying pan, heat the avocado oil over high heat until you see ripples. Carefully place the fillets in the pan, skin-side down. Press down gently with a flat spatula for 30 seconds to prevent the fillets from curling up when the skin contracts. Cook undisturbed until the bottom half turns opaque and the fillets can move freely when the pan is shaken, 2–3 minutes.

3. Flip the fish carefully with a flat spatula, taking care not to break it apart. (You can press a spoon on the flesh side to prevent the fish from moving while you slide the spatula under the skin side.) Press down with the spatula for a few seconds to let the fish come into contact with the pan. Cook until the flesh side just turns opaque, 1–2 minutes. Remove to a plate and set skin-side up. (Don't overcook it. The fish will continue to cook after it's out of the pan.)

4. Add the leek to the oil remaining in the pan. Cook over medium heat, stirring occasionally, until softened, 2–3 minutes. Add the wine and the remaining pinch of salt and stir to combine.

5. Divide the baby greens among four plates. Top with the leek and then the seared fish. Drizzle the lemon juice around (but not on) the fish to keep the crispness of the skin. Sprinkle with the pepper and serve with the lemon wedges, if desired.

Note: This cooking method ensures a crispy skin. If you move the fish too soon, the skin will stick to the pan and separate from the flesh. If you're inexperienced with cooking fish, you may want to sear in batches because it is difficult to take care of more than two pieces of fish at a time.

→ *Pairs with* ←
A grain dish and ② vegetable or salad dishes for a complete meal.

Salt and Vinegar Broiled Spanish Mackerel

Spanish mackerel is among the fish with the highest amount of omega-3 fatty acids, with about 1 gram per 4-ounce (120 g) serving. Omega-3 fatty acids are anti-inflammatory and good for cardiovascular health. Mackerel is high in lean protein and full of flavor. The coriander seeds and stems complement those rich flavors.

Preparation time: 10 minutes
Cooking time: 15 minutes
Serves 4

* 2 teaspoons white wine vinegar or distilled white vinegar
* 2 skin-on Spanish mackerel fillets (about 8 oz/225 g each), halved crosswise (see *Note*)
* ½ teaspoon coarse sea salt
* 1 teaspoon coriander seeds
* 1 tablespoon chopped cilantro (coriander) stems
* 4 cloves garlic, peeled
* 4 teaspoons olive oil
* Lemon wedges for serving (optional)

1. Preheat the oven to 450°F (230°C/Gas Mark 8).

2. Meanwhile, sprinkle the vinegar on the flesh side of the fillets, then sprinkle with ¼ teaspoon of the salt. Let marinate for 5 minutes.

3. In a mortar and postle (or spice grinder), crush and grind the coriander seeds, cilantro (coriander) stems, and garlic to a paste. Spread the paste on the flesh side of the fillets.

4. Brush a sheet pan with 2 teaspoons of the oil. Lay the fillets flesh-side down in the pan. Drizzle the remaining 2 teaspoons oil on the skin side. Sprinkle with the remaining ¼ teaspoon salt.

5. Roast until cooked through and the edges of the skin are slightly browned, 10–15 minutes. Serve with lemon wedges, if desired.

Note: If Spanish mackerel fillets are not available, use regular mackerel fillets, which are smaller (about 4 oz/120 g each). They are thinner, too, requiring less cooking time.

> → *Pairs with* ←
> A grain dish and 2
> vegetable or salad dishes
> for a complete meal.

Honey-Glazed Mahi-mahi with Parsley

Mahi-mahi, also called dolphinfish or dorado, produces fillets that are substantial, firm, and mild in flavor. It is a good source of healthy, lean marine protein. I like to add a little triple sec or Grand Marnier liqueur to the cooking wine to bring some interesting flavors to the dish. In addition to the wine, I use honey to glaze the fish, making it a little high in sugar, but it tastes delicious and is still under the 25 grams of added sugar per day limit. If microgreens are not readily available where you live, you can buy a kit to sprout them at home—they grow fast and make a refreshing garnish for so many dishes.

Preparation time: 10 minutes
Cooking time: 20 minutes
Serves 4
For gluten-free, use gluten-free tamari

* 4 skinless mahi-mahi fillets (about 6 oz/175 g each), 1 inch/2.5 cm thick
* ½ teaspoon kosher (flaked) salt
* ½ teaspoon freshly ground black pepper
* ½ teaspoon chopped thyme
* ½ teaspoon sweet paprika
* ¼ cup (2 fl oz/60 ml) olive oil
* 4–8 cloves garlic, chopped, to taste
* ½ cup (4 fl oz/120 ml) white wine or rice wine
* 1 teaspoon triple sec, Grand Marnier, or other orange-flavored liqueur
* 6 tablespoons honey
* ¼ cup (2 fl oz/60 ml) soy sauce or gluten-free tamari
* 2 tablespoons vinegar (white vinegar for a clean taste or balsamic vinegar for a stronger taste)
* 2 tablespoons chopped parsley and/or dill
* Handful of microgreens, for garnish

1. Preheat the broiler (grill) to low. Pat the fish fillets dry with paper towels. Rub both sides with the salt, pepper, thyme, and paprika.

2. In a large ovenproof frying pan, heat the olive oil over medium heat. Add the garlic and cook until fragrant, about 1 minute. Add the wine, triple sec, honey, ¼ cup (2 fl oz/60 ml) water, soy sauce, and vinegar. Bring to a boil and stir to combine.

3. Add the fish fillets and simmer for 1 minute. Use a spoon to scoop up the liquid and baste the fillets for 1–2 minutes.

4. Transfer the pan to the oven and broil (grill) on low until the fish starts to flake, about 5 minutes (or longer if the fillets are thicker). Remove the pan from the broiler and increase the broiler heat to high. Tilt the pan away from you and baste again, then broil until the fillets are nicely glazed, about 2 minutes.

5. Let the fish rest out of the oven for 5 minutes, then transfer to serving plates.

6. Bring the juices in the pan to a boil and cook until syrupy then pour over the fish. Sprinkle with the parsley and garnish with the microgreens.

> → *Pairs with* ←
> A grain dish and 2
> vegetable or salad dishes
> for a complete meal.

Steamed Whole Branzino with Scallions and Ginger

Steaming is a very healthy cooking method. It cooks the food quickly without burning or drying it out, preserving the nutrients. This cooking method demands the freshest raw ingredients, for it showcases the original flavors of the fish without adding much else. (If fish is not super fresh, pan-frying or baking can mask some imperfections.) However, it is easy to overcook fish when steaming. To prevent that, stop as soon as the flesh has turned opaque, remove from the steamer, and let it finish cooking from the residual heat. Using a steamer with a glass lid makes it easier to observe the fish while cooking.

Preparation time: ①◎ minutes
Cooking time: ①◎ minutes
Serves ④
For gluten-free, use gluten-free tamari

* 1 whole branzino (about 2 lb/900 g), scaled and cleaned
* 2 scallions (spring onions)
* 1 tablespoon distilled white vinegar or rice vinegar
* ¼ cup (25 g) sliced fresh ginger
* ¼ cup (2 fl oz/60 ml) slightly sweet white wine, such as Moscato or white rice wine
* ¼ teaspoon fine sea salt
* 2 tablespoons mild-flavored oil, such as canola (rapeseed) oil
* Pinch of sesame seeds
* 1 tablespoon soy sauce or gluten-free tamari

1. Rinse the fish clean. Remove any residual scales and the black membrane inside the belly, if present. Make 2 or 3 cuts across the meaty part of the fish on each side, about ½ inch (1.25 cm) deep to allow the flavors of the spices to penetrate the fish. Remove the head if desired.

2. Cut the white part of the scallions (spring onions) into 1-inch (2.5 cm) lengths. Finely chop the greens.

3. Set the fish on a large plate that fits in your steamer. Rub half of the vinegar in the inner wall of the fish's belly and the remaining half over the skin. Put two lengths of scallion white and a slice of ginger in the belly. Put a few lengths of scallion white and a few slices of ginger underneath the fish, and the remainder on top. Drizzle the wine on top and then sprinkle with the salt. (If the whole fish is too long to fit in the steamer, you can cut it in half crosswise so it fits.)

4. Bring the water to a boil in the bottom of a steamer. Once boiling, place the plate with the fish in the steamer. Cover and steam over high heat, just until the flesh exposed from the cutting in the first step becomes opaque, 5–7 minutes. Don't overcook it.

5. Remove the plate from the steamer immediately and let it cool gradually to room temperature on the countertop.

6. In a small saucepan, heat the canola oil over high heat until very hot but not smoking. Add the sesame seeds to the oil and cook until the seeds have turned golden, 2 minutes. Meanwhile, pile the scallion greens on top of the fish. When the sesame seeds and oil are ready. pour on top of the scallion greens. You should hear a sizzling sound and smell the scallion fragrance.

7. Drizzle the soy sauce on top of the fish. Use a spoon to scoop up the juices on the plate and drizzle over the top of the fish. When serving, remove the flesh from the bone and drizzle with the sauce.

> → *Pairs with* ←
> A grain dish and ②
> vegetable or salad dishes
> for a complete meal.

Pil-Pil Haddock

Pil-pil is a Basque sauce made from the emulsified mixture of cooking juices and olive oil. Traditionally, the dish was made with salt cod because of lack of refrigeration. Here, I use fresh fish, as it doesn't have as much salt and the protein is fresher. You can use either haddock or Atlantic cod for this dish. The key is the slow cooking at low heat and frequent shaking and basting movements, which produce the characteristic sauce. This dish should be a little spicy for the full experience. It does use more oil per serving than other dishes in this book, so eat once in a while for a treat.

Preparation time: ①⓪ minutes
Cooking time: ①⑤ minutes
Serves ④

* 4 haddock fillets (about 6 oz/ 175 g each)
* 1 tablespoon fresh lemon juice
* ½ teaspoon kosher (flaked) salt
* ½ cup (4 fl oz/120 ml) extra-virgin olive oil
* 8 cloves garlic, sliced
* ¼ teaspoon sweet paprika
* ¼ cup (40 g) chopped Italian frying peppers (cubanelles) or shishito peppers
* ¼–1 teaspoon crushed chili flakes or cayenne pepper, depending on your taste for heat

1. In a shallow bowl, combine the fish, lemon juice, and salt and let marinate for 5 minutes.

2. In a large frying pan, heat the olive oil over medium-low heat. Add the garlic and cook until fragrant, 1–2 minutes. Remove the garlic with a spoon and set aside.

3. Reduce the heat to low. Add the fish and marinade. Shake the pan gently back and forth frequently so the fish and juices move around the pan. (This movement combines the juices and the olive oil to emulsify them.) Baste the fish from time to time with a spoon. Eventually you will hear the crackly "pil pil" sound that the juices and oil make—the namesake of the dish.

4. Once the fish start to flake, about 10 minutes depending on thickness, flip them carefully so they don't break up. Return the cooked garlic to the pan and add the paprika, Italian peppers, and chili flakes alongside the fish. Continue cooking and shaking the pan as above until the fish is completely cooked through, 2–4 minutes more.

5. Transfer the fish to serving plates. The juices should have thickened to a somewhat opaque emulsion. If not, beat them with a spoon or whisk to thicken and emulsify. Pour the sauce over the fish and serve.

> → *Pairs with* ←
> A grain dish and ②
> vegetable or salad dishes
> for a complete meal.

Lemon-Garlic Baked Cod

Cod is a white fish with flaky flesh. Although it doesn't have as much omega-3 fatty acids (the healthy fat) as salmon, it is readily available and a good source of high-quality protein. Cod can be cooked many ways. Here, I keep it simple, just coated with a few flavorful seasonings and baked for a quick, delicious, and nutritious dish.

Preparation time: ⑤ minutes
Cooking time: ①⑤ minutes
Serves ④

* 4 skinless cod fillets (5–6 oz/150–175 g each), 1½ inches (4 cm) thick
* ½ teaspoon kosher (flaked) salt
* ¼ teaspoon freshly ground black pepper
* 1 teaspoon cornstarch (cornflour)
* ¼ cup (2 fl oz/60 ml) extra virgin olive oil
* Juice of ¼ lemon, plus wedges for serving (optional)
* 2 cloves garlic, minced
* Pinch of sweet paprika (optional)
* Pinch of cayenne pepper (optional)

1. Preheat the oven to 400°F (200°C/ Gas Mark 6).

2. Dry the cod with paper towels. Sprinkle with the salt and black pepper, then dust with the cornstarch (cornflour).

3. In an 8 × 8-inch (20 × 20 cm) glass baking dish (which should hold all the fillets with some space in between), combine the olive oil, lemon juice, and garlic.

4. Add the fish and turn to coat in the olive oil mixture. If desired, sprinkle with paprika and/or cayenne. Scoop up some of the minced garlic and spread on top of the fish.

5. Bake until the fish flakes easily with a fork, about 10 minutes, depending on thickness. Remove from the oven and let rest at room temperature for 5 minutes before serving with lemon wedges alongside, if desired.

> → *Pairs with* ←
> A grain dish and ②
> vegetable or salad dishes
> for a complete meal.

Aioli Shrimp with Walnuts

Shrimp (prawns) are a good source of marine protein, and walnuts are rich in plant protein and plant oil. This combination serves as a healthy protein dish that pairs well with light-tasting vegetables and carbohydrates. You may be aware that shrimp is high in cholesterol, but there is "bad" cholesterol (LDL, low density lipoprotein), which can cause damage to the body, and "good" cholesterol (HDL, high density lipoprotein), which helps the body remove the bad cholesterol. Shrimp in moderate amounts was found to actually raise the levels of good cholesterol (HDL) more than the bad cholesterol (LDL). Look for shrimp with translucent and firm flesh, which indicates freshness. It is easy to overcook shrimp, which will make them hard and dry. Shrimp that are fresh and properly cooked should feel almost crunchy when you eat them. In the dish, I prefer the healthier homemade aioli over mayonnaise because it uses olive oil. The milk powder adds creaminess to the dressing, but you can omit it if you don't have it.

Preparation time: 10 minutes
Cooking time: 10 minutes
Serves 4
For dairy-free, omit the milk powder

* 16 shrimp (prawns), peeled and deveined
* ½ teaspoon kosher (flaked) salt
* 1 teaspoon cornstarch (cornflour)
* Pinch of freshly ground white pepper or black pepper
* ¼ cup (2 fl oz/60 ml) olive oil
* 1 cup (150 g) walnuts
* 2 tablespoons honey
* 2 scallions (spring onions), cut into 1-inch (2.5 cm) lengths
* 2 tablespoons aioli (from Red Cabbage Coleslaw, page 94) or mayonnaise
* 1 teaspoon milk powder (optional)
* 2 tablespoons chopped parsley

1. In a medium bowl, combine the shrimp (prawns), salt, cornstarch (cornflour), and pepper. Mix well to coat each shrimp.

2. In a large frying pan, heat the olive oil over medium-low heat. Add the walnuts and fry until lightly browned, stirring occasionally, about 2 minutes. Transfer the walnuts to a bowl, add the honey, and toss to coat the walnuts.

3. Increase the heat under the frying pan to medium. Add the shrimp and scallion (spring onion) segments to the oil remaining in the pan. Cook, stirring occasionally, until opaque and cooked through, about 3 minutes. Remove to a serving bowl.

4. Add the aioli to the bowl and sprinkle with the milk powder (if using). Toss to mix well. Add the walnuts and toss again. Sprinkle with the parsley.

> → *Pairs with* ←
> A grain dish and 2
> vegetable or salad dishes
> for a complete meal.

Seared Scallops

Scallops are pure, packed marine protein—a good substitute for poultry or meat. They have a sweet and delicate flavor, but hold their shape when cooked. Make sure you buy "dry-packed" scallops for this dish. "Wet-packed" scallops (often frozen) have been soaked in a solution to make them moist, which means that during the cooking process, water will seep out and the scallops won't brown. I like to use avocado oil for searing because of its high smoke point.

Preparation time: ⑩ minutes
Cooking time: ⑤ minutes
Serves ④

* 1 lb (450 g) dry-packed scallops
* ¼ teaspoon coarse sea salt
* Pinch of freshly ground white pepper
* 1 tablespoon avocado oil
* 4 tablespoons mirin (or 4 tablespoons white wine mixed with 1 teaspoon sugar)
* 1 tablespoon chopped chives or scallions (spring onions)

1. Dry the scallops well with paper towels. Sprinkle the tops of the scallops with the salt and pepper.

2. In a large frying pan, heat the oil over high heat. When the pan is very hot, lay the scallops in the pan with salted-side down. Don't overcrowd. Reduce the heat and sear, without moving them, over medium heat until browned, about 2 minutes. Flip the scallops. Sear until browned on the second side, about 1½ minutes.

3. Remove from the heat and add the mirin. Baste the scallops with a spoon and use the residual heat in the pan to cook down the liquid until it is no longer bubbling.

4. Transfer to serving plates and sprinkle with the chives.

> ⇝ *Pairs with* ⇜
> A grain dish and ②
> vegetable or salad dishes
> for a complete meal.

Steamed Mussels with White Wine

Mussels are low in fat and carbohydrates but high in protein. They are also rich in micronutrients such as zinc, manganese, and selenium. I like to cook them in the simplest way possible—just steam them in their own brine with some wine and lemon juice to enhance the flavor. This makes a quick protein dish for lunch or dinner. No salt is needed in this recipe, as the mussels release their brine.

Preparation time: 15 minutes
Cooking time: 10 minutes
Serves 4
For dairy-free, omit the butter

* 1 tablespoon olive oil
* 1 tablespoon finely chopped shallot or onion
* 4 cloves garlic, minced
* 2 lb (900 g) mussels (see *Note*), thoroughly scrubbed and debearded
* 1 cup (8 fl oz/250 ml) light dry white wine, such as Sauvignon Blanc or Pinot Grigio
* 1 tablespoon roughly chopped parsley
* 1 lemon, the middle third cut into 4 slices and the rest squeezed for juice
* 1 tablespoon (15 g) unsalted butter (optional)

1. In a large pot, heat the olive oil over medium heat. Add the shallot and garlic and cook, stirring, until fragrant, 1–2 minutes.

2. Add the mussels, wine, parsley, and lemon juice. Increase the heat to high, cover, and cook until the mussels have opened, 3–5 minutes. Toss them a little so that any that have not opened due to crowding have a chance to fully open. Cook, covered, for 1 more minute.

3. Transfer the mussels to four large bowls. Discard any mussels that have not opened.

4. Add the butter (if using) to the broth in the pan and stir to melt. Pour the broth over the top of the mussels. (There may be some grit left in the broth so take care to leave it behind.) Garnish with lemon slices.

Note: When buying mussels, choose those that are closed or quickly close when tapped, otherwise they should be discarded. If the mussels came in a bag and you couldn't examine each one, also look for any that might be broken open and discard those. If a mussel doesn't open after cooking, discard it, too.

> → *Pairs with* ←
> A grain dish and 2
> vegetable or salad dishes
> for a complete meal.

Monkfish Stew with Red Sauce

Monkfish has firm, white flesh and a very mild flavor. It is a good protein source, and is sometimes called "the poor man's lobster" because it has a similar texture and taste when cooked correctly, yet is much less expensive. Because its flesh is firm, it can withstand some handling and won't break apart as other fish does—lending itself to the cooking method in this recipe. If monkfish is not available, any firm fish, such as swordfish or halibut, can be used as a substitute. Tomato, paprika, and saffron give this dish a brilliant color and savory taste—just like a lobster tail.

Preparation time: ①⓪ minutes
Cooking time: ②⓪ minutes
Serves ④

* ½ teaspoon saffron threads
* 2 skinned monkfish tails (12–16 oz/340–450 g each), each tail cut crosswise to create 4 medallions 2 inches (5 cm) thick
* ½ teaspoon kosher (flaked) salt
* ¼ cup (30 g) whole-wheat flour
* 6 tablespoons olive oil
* 8 cloves garlic, sliced
* 3 medium tomatoes, thinly sliced into rounds
* 2 teaspoons tomato paste (tomato purée)
* 1 teaspoon sweet paprika
* 1 cup (8 fl oz/250 ml) dry or semi-dry white wine, such as Chablis
* Microgreens (optional), for garnish

1. Put the saffron in a small bowl and add a few teaspoons of water. Let steep for 5 minutes.

2. Sprinkle the monkfish with the salt and let sit for 5 minutes. Pat the fish dry with paper towels. Spread the flour on a plate, then dredge the fish on all sides with a thin coating of flour. Reserve the 1 or 2 tablespoons flour remaining on the plate.

3. In a large frying pan that can hold the fish medallions in a single layer, heat the oil over medium heat. Pan-fry the monkfish until lightly browned, about 2 minutes. Flip and brown the other side, about 2 minutes. Turn the medallions as needed to brown the sides.

4. Add the garlic and cook until fragrant, about 1 minute. Add the tomatoes and tomato paste (purée) and cook until softened, about 1 minute. Add the paprika, saffron and soaking water, the wine, and 1 cup (8 fl oz/250 ml) water. Bring to a simmer, cover, and cook until saucy, about 3 minutes. Flip the fish, taking care not to break up the medallions. Simmer until the fish is almost cooked through, 2–4 minutes.

5. In a small bowl, stir the flour left over from coating the fish in 1 cup (8 fl oz/250 ml) water. Whisk this slurry into the sauce, cover, and simmer until the sauce is thickened, about 2 minutes.

6. Transfer the monkfish to serving bowls and ladle the sauce over the top. If desired, garnish with microgreens.

> → Pairs with ←
> A grain dish and ②
> vegetable or salad dishes
> for a complete meal.

Basic Bone Broth

Bone broth was traditionally made as a way of extracting nutrients from discarded bones when meat was a luxury. The slow cooking brings out the collagen (a protein abundant in skin, cartilage, and bone) and breaks some of it down into peptides and amino acids, which are reused by the body to make connective tissues. The acidity from the sauerkraut helps convert the proteins to these umami-producing peptides and amino acids. It also helps release calcium from the bones into the broth. Meat and bone cooked this way release their nutrients in ways that are easy to digest and absorb. Bone broth differs from meat stock in that it is made using more bones than meat and takes many hours to cook. I use a blanching technique to remove the loose debris that comes with the bones to create a clear and clean-tasting broth. Because it takes so long to make, I've scaled it up to eight servings.

Preparation time: ① hour
Cooking time: ④ hours to overnight
Serves: ⑧

* 4 lb (1.8 kg) beef bones, pork bones, or chicken bones (see *Note 1*), cut into 4-inch (10 cm) pieces
* ¼ cup (2 fl oz/60 ml) light-colored cooking wine, such as white wine or rice wine
* ¼ teaspoon black peppercorns
* ¼ teaspoon fennel seeds
* ¼ teaspoon coriander seeds
* ¼ teaspoon mustard seeds
* ¼ teaspoon fenugreek seeds
* 3 allspice berries
* 2 green cardamom pods
* 1 star anise
* 2 bay leaves
* 2 cloves garlic, peeled and whole
* 2-inch piece (25 g) fresh ginger
* 2 scallions (spring onions) or ½ medium onion
* 8 oz (225 g) sauerkraut with brine
* Fine sea salt, to taste

1. Soak the bones in cold water for 30 minutes to release any trapped blood. Rinse several times until the water is clear.

2. For a brown (not clear) broth, roast the bones first, if desired; see *Note 2*.

3. Fill a large pot with enough cold water to submerge the bones. Bring the water to a boil over high heat, then add the bones and wine and cook over high heat until any meat left on the bones turns pale, 2–3 minutes. Pour out the hot water and rinse the bones with several rounds of cold water, until all loose debris is gone. Return the bones to the pot and add cold water to cover by 2–4 inches (5–10 cm). Enclose the peppercorns, fennel seeds, coriander seeds, mustard seeds, fenugreek seeds, allspice, cardamom, and star anise in a tea ball (or tie in a square of cheesecloth). Add the infusion ball, bay leaves, garlic, ginger, scallions (spring onions), and sauerkraut. Bring to a boil over high heat, then reduce the heat to a bare simmer, cover, and cook for 4–10 hours, the longer the better. (You can also do this in the oven: see *Note 3*.)

4. Strain the finished broth into another pot. If you want to remove the fat, let the broth cool to room temperature, then chill in the refrigerator until the fat on the top of the soup is set. Remove the fat. If you would prefer to emulsify the fat into the broth, boil the broth vigorously for 20 minutes at the end of the cooking.

5. When ready to serve (depending on how you are using it), salt the broth to taste. It can be consumed as is like a consommé or can be used as a stock when sautéing or braising foods, or as a substitute for water when cooking grains. It also serves as a rich base for soups

(see *Note 4*). The broth can be stored in the refrigerator for 1 or 2 days and in the freezer for a few weeks.

Note 1: Get the bones from the butcher, after they have removed whatever cuts of meat they are from. Look for shoulder and/or neck, back, or tail. Avoid the leg/shank bones as they contain too much greasy marrow. You can also use chicken bones—leg bones, backs, or the whole frame.

Note 2: For a brown (not clear) broth, roast the cleaned bones at 400°F (200°C/Gas Mark 6) for 30 minutes before making the broth.

Note 3: To slow-roast the broth: Set the covered pot in a 200–225°F (93–107°C/Gas Mark ¼) oven overnight, 8–12 hours. This slow-cooking process will really get the meat and cartilage falling off the bones and release even more nutrients into the broth.

Note 4: To make a simple vegetable stew/soup, boil chunky vegetables (carrots, turnips, celery, daikon radish, pumpkin, or butternut squash) in the bone broth for 30 minutes, or leafy vegetables (spinach, kale, Swiss chard, turnip greens, watercress) for 1 minute. Or use it as a base for other soups or stews, such as minestrone, corn bisque, or goulash.

> This can be consumed as a beverage or used as a broth for other dishes. It can pair with a protein dish, a grain dish, and ② vegetable dishes for a complete meal.

Stewed Chicken

Chicken is a popular source of protein and adaptable to many cooking methods—stewing, baking, sautéing, and steaming are all healthier than frying. To further reduce intake of animal fat, remove the skin. Pasture-raised chickens are raised in an environment most resembling their natural habitat, with the chickens allowed to roam around the field finding seeds, insects, and worms—their natural diet. Get pasture-raised chicken whenever you can as you will find the meat more flavorful. This dish is a tribute to the best chicken I ever had, which was on a Caribbean island—it was very fresh, juicy, and intensely flavorful, even with minimal seasoning.

Preparation time: ①⑤ minutes
Cooking time: ③◎ minutes
Serves ④

* 4 tablespoons extra-virgin olive oil
* 2 teaspoons sugar
* 2 lb (900 g) boneless, skinless chicken thighs or breasts, cut into 2-inch (5 cm) pieces
* 2 medium red onions, chopped
* 1 stalk celery, chopped
* 4 cloves garlic, sliced
* 1 lb (450 g) tomatoes, chopped
* 1 red bell pepper, cut into 1-inch (2.5 cm) squares
* 2 teaspoons dried oregano or 4 teaspoons chopped fresh
* 2 bay leaves
* ¼ cup (2 fl oz/60 ml) white wine
* 2 tablespoons fresh lime juice
* ½ teaspoon coarse sea salt
* 8 pitted green olives
* 1 cup (30 g) chopped cilantro (coriander)
* ½ teaspoon freshly ground black pepper

1. In a large frying pan, heat the olive oil over medium heat. Add the sugar and stir until caramelized, 2–3 minutes. Add the chicken, stir, and cook undisturbed in a single layer to caramelize the chicken, about 1 minute. Flip the chicken and caramelize the other side, about 1 minute. Remove the chicken to a plate and set aside.

2. To the same pan, add the onions, celery, and garlic and cook until fragrant, 2–3 minutes. Add the tomatoes, bell pepper, oregano, bay leaves, wine, lime juice, and salt. Simmer until the tomato and pepper soften, 3–5 minutes. Stir in the chicken and olives. Reduce the heat to low, cover, and simmer until the chicken is cooked through, about 20 minutes for thighs, a few minutes less for breasts.

3. Sprinkle with the cilantro (coriander) and black pepper and serve.

⇥ *Pairs with* ⇤
A grain dish and ② vegetable or salad dishes for a complete meal.

Cashew Chicken

Chicken breast is full of lean protein, however it's often battered and deep fried, or rubbed with spices and grilled. Although crispy skin tastes good, it is loaded with oil, salt, and fried starch—not a healthy combination. Open-flame grilling is also not the healthiest cooking method. This dish of tender chicken breast, crunchy nuts, and crisp fresh vegetables is both tasty and healthy. The secret is in the light dusting of cornstarch (cornflour) on the chicken pieces, which seals in the flavor and moisture to keep the chicken juicy, plus the savory sauce that coats all the ingredients and brings the dish together. Use pasture-raised chicken if you can, as it's more flavorful and richer in micronutrients because the chickens' diet is more diverse.

Preparation time: 20 minutes
Cooking time: 10 minutes
Serves 4

* 1 cup (150 g) cashews
* 4 boneless, skinless chicken breasts (4–6 oz/120–175 g each), cut into 1-inch (2.5 cm) cubes
* 1 teaspoon toasted sesame oil
* ¼ teaspoon kosher (flaked) salt
* ¼ teaspoon freshly ground black pepper
* ¼ teaspoon grated fresh ginger
* 1 tablespoon rice wine
* 1 tablespoon mirin or honey
* 1 teaspoon white wine vinegar or apple cider vinegar
* 1 tablespoon soy sauce
* 2 tablespoons hoisin sauce or oyster sauce
* 2 cloves garlic, minced
* 4 teaspoons cornstarch (cornflour)
* 4 tablespoons olive oil
* 1 large onion, cut into 1-inch (2.5 cm) chunks
* 1 red bell pepper, cut into 1-inch (2.5 cm) chunks
* 1 green bell pepper, cut into 1-inch (2.5 cm) chunks
* 2 cups broccoli florets, cut into 1–2-inch (2.5–5 cm) pieces
* 1 scallion (spring onion), chopped
* 2 teaspoons toasted sesame seeds

1. Preheat the oven to 350°F (180°C/ Gas Mark 4).

2. Spread the cashews in a single layer on a baking sheet and toast until golden and fragrant, about 5 minutes. Remove and let cool.

3. In a bowl, toss the chicken with the sesame oil, salt, pepper, and ginger. Let marinate for 10 minutes.

4. In a small bowl, whisk together the rice wine, mirin, vinegar, soy sauce, hoisin, garlic, and 2 teaspoons of the cornstarch (cornflour). Set the sauce aside.

5. When you're ready to cook, sprinkle the remaining 2 teaspoons cornstarch over the chicken and massage it in evenly. (Do this right before cooking. Leaving the starch on the chicken for too long will cause the starch to dissolve and it will become soggy.)

6. In a large frying pan, heat 2 tablespoons of the olive oil over medium heat until it ripples. Add half the chicken, spread in a single layer, and cook until golden, about 1 minute. Toss and cook until all sides are golden, 2–3 minutes. Remove and set aside in a large bowl or plate. Repeat with the remaining 2 tablespoons olive oil and chicken. (Cooking the chicken in batches prevents overcrowding and steaming of the chicken.)

7. Add the onion to the oil left in the pan and cook, stirring, until fragrant, about 1 minute. Add the bell peppers and broccoli, stirring to thoroughly coat in the oil, 1–2 minutes. Remove and combine with the chicken.

8. Whisk the sauce again, add to the pan, and simmer until it starts to thicken, 1–2 minutes. Return the vegetables and chicken to the pan and stir evenly to coat. Return to a simmer, then stir in the cashews.

9. Serve sprinkled with the chopped scallion (spring onion) and toasted sesame seeds.

> → *Pairs with* ←
> A grain dish and 2
> vegetable or salad dishes
> for a complete meal.

Slow-Roasted Turkey Breast

It can be easy to make roasted turkey dry. Brining helps flavor to penetrate the meat, but it takes a long time. You can avoid both of these problems with this recipe. The secret is in cooking it at a lower temperature for a longer time—a foolproof method to keep meats juicy and tender. At a temperature just below boiling point, the moisture doesn't leave the meat but will still cook it through. Plan the long cooking time to fit your schedule. This dish can be prepared in the morning, cooked during the day, and ready for dinner. Or prepared in the evening, cooked overnight, and ready in the morning for a packed lunch. It requires minimal preparation time, only about 5 minutes. Rub, seal, put in the oven, and forget about it.

Preparation time: ⑤ minutes
Cooking time: ⑥–⑧ hours
Serves ④

* 1 lb 8 oz (680 g) boneless turkey breast, with skin or skinless, in one piece
* Juice of ½ lemon
* 1 teaspoon kosher (flaked) salt
* ¼ teaspoon freshly ground black pepper
* ¼ teaspoon ground sumac
* ¼ teaspoon advieh spice blend (see *Note 1*)
* ½ medium onion, sliced
* 1 tablespoon honey (optional)
* 1–2 teaspoons cornstarch (cornflour), for thickening (optional)
* 1 tablespoon chopped parsley, for garnish

1. Put the turkey breast skin-side up in a ceramic or metal baking dish that is slightly larger than the turkey breast and 1–2 inches (2.5–5 cm) deep. Sprinkle the lemon juice on both sides of the turkey breast. Rub evenly with the salt and pepper. Sprinkle the sumac and advieh on both sides. Arrange the onion slices on top. Cover with foil and seal the rim so it is almost airtight (see *Note 2*).

2. Position a rack in the center of the oven and preheat the oven to 200°F (93°C/ Gas Mark ¼) (see *Note 3*).

3. Transfer the turkey to the oven and slow-roast until the turkey is meltingly tender, 6–8 hours. If you'd like crispy skin, brush the honey onto the skin and broil (grill) under high heat.

4. Remove to a carving board. Slice the turkey breast across the grain. Spoon the pan juices over the sliced turkey. (If you'd like a thicker sauce, whisk the cornstarch/cornflour into the pan juices and simmer until thickened, 1–2 minutes.) Sprinkle with the parsley and serve.

Note 1: Advieh is a Persian spice mix that gives this dish a Middle Eastern flavor. It is made of several aromatic spices. The exact composition can vary from kitchen to kitchen—there is no gold standard. If you want to make it yourself, grind 1 part cloves, 2 parts black pepper, 2 parts dried lime strips, 2 parts nutmeg, 4 parts dried rose petals (these can be hard to find; use dried rose buds if necessary), 4 parts green cardamom, 4 parts ground turmeric, 8 parts cinnamon, and 8 parts cumin seeds. Store in an airtight container kept in a dark and cool place.

Note 2: If you have the time, and for an even richer flavor, you could leave the turkey to marinate at this point for up to 8 hours before cooking.

Note 3: If your oven doesn't go as low as 200°F (93°C/Gas Mark ¼), just cook at the lowest temperature option you have available and check the turkey for doneness about 1 hour earlier.

> ⇢ *Pairs with* ⇠
> A grain dish and ②
> vegetable or salad dishes
> for a complete meal.

Turkey Meatballs
with Tomato Sauce

Meatballs are a comfort food dish for many families, but the traditional recipe calls for the use of red meat. To make them healthier, here I use ground turkey breast, add more eggs, and use chopped mushroom and sourdough breadcrumbs for enhanced umami. When cooking turkey, adding a little bit of sugar will create the Maillard reaction and deepen the flavor. I also use crushed grapes as a source of sugar and fruity flavor, but you can also use a little regular sugar. This dish can be served on top of pasta or by itself as a protein dish.

Preparation time: ②⑤ minutes
Cooking time: ②◎ minutes
Serves ④
For dairy-free, omit the cheese

* 6 tablespoons extra-virgin olive oil
* ½ cup (45 g) chopped white or portobello mushrooms
* 1 medium onion, chopped
* 4 cloves garlic, chopped
* 1 lb (450 g) ground (minced) turkey breast
* 3 eggs
* ½ cup (15 g) chopped parsley
* Leaves of 1 sprig oregano, chopped
* 1½ teaspoons coarse sea salt
* 1½ cups (105 g) loosely packed fresh sourdough breadcrumbs (coarsely ground from 2–3 slices sourdough bread)
* 1 lb (450 g) plum tomatoes, thinly sliced
* 6 seedless grapes, crushed, or 1 teaspoon sugar
* 1 teaspoon Italian tomato paste (tomato purée), preferably from a tube
* ¼ cup (5 g) picked basil leaves
* 1 teaspoon grated Parmigiano-Reggiano cheese (optional)

1. In a small saucepan, bring 2 cups (16 fl oz/475 ml) water to just below a simmer.

2. In a large frying pan, heat 2 tablespoons of the olive oil over medium heat. Add the mushrooms, half the onion, and half the garlic. Cook until the mushrooms and onions are browned, about 2 minutes. Remove to a large bowl and let cool.

3. To the large bowl, add the ground turkey, eggs, parsley, oregano, and 1 teaspoon of the salt. Mix well with your hands, adding enough of the breadcrumbs to make a mixture firm enough to form into balls. Roll into 2-inch (5 cm) meatballs, about 16 of them.

4. In the same frying pan, heat 2 tablespoons of the olive oil over medium heat. Pan-fry the meatballs for a few minutes until browned, then flip and fry the other side until browned. Set aside on a plate.

5. Add the remaining 2 tablespoons oil and the remaining chopped garlic and onion to the pan. Cook until fragrant, about 1 minute. Arrange the sliced tomatoes on top, sprinkle with the remaining ½ teaspoon salt and the crushed grapes. Cover and cook over medium heat until the tomatoes soften and start to break apart, about 2 minutes.

6. Stir in the hot water and tomato paste, re-cover, and simmer over medium-low heat until the tomato slices break down, about 5 minutes. Mix in the meatballs, cover, and simmer until the meatballs are cooked through, another 5 minutes. Remove from the heat and sprinkle with the basil and Parmigiano (if using).

Note: Having a pot of boiling water on standby is very handy when cooking. When adding water to a dish, add hot water rather than room temperature water. The sudden change in temperature from adding cooler water can coagulate some of the substances in the dish and make it lose flavor. When adding hot water, as in this recipe, you will find that the sauce preserves more of the umami taste from the tomato. I use an electric kettle, which is more energy efficient and can heat up the water very fast. It also does not take up any room on the stovetop.

→ *Pairs with* ←
A grain dish and ②
vegetable or salad dishes
for a complete meal.

Beef Stew with Carrots, Cauliflower, and Cabbage

Eating too much red meat isn't good for you. However, an occasional red meat dish (once or twice a month) is fine in a mostly plant-based diet. I prefer a low-temperature cooking method, such as stewing or braising, instead of grilling or frying. Here, I adapt a classic beef stew recipe to make it healthier. Instead of potato, which has a high glycemic index and is starchy, I use cauliflower and cabbage, healthy cruciferous vegetables, plus green peas, with the classic carrots. I also use a much higher vegetable to meat ratio, to bring the proportions to the healthy range.

Preparation time: 20 minutes
Cooking time: about 3 hours
Serves 4
For gluten-free, use cornstarch (cornflour)

* ¼ cup (35 g) all-purpose flour or 2 tablespoons cornstarch (cornflour)
* 1 teaspoon sugar
* ¼ teaspoon freshly ground black pepper
* ½ teaspoon sea salt, plus extra for seasoning
* 1½ lb (680 g) boneless beef chuck (roast), cut into 1½-inch (4 cm) cubes
* 2 tablespoons olive oil
* 1 stalk celery, chopped
* 2 large carrots—1 cut into 2-inch (5 cm) lengths, 1 cut into 1-inch (2.5 cm) chunks
* ½ medium onion, chopped
* 2 cloves garlic, chopped
* 2 cups (16 fl oz/475 ml) stock (beef, chicken, or vegetable) or water, plus more as needed
* 1 cup (8 fl oz/250 ml) dry red wine
* 2 tablespoons balsamic vinegar
* 1 tablespoon tomato paste (tomato purée)
* 2 bay leaves
* 1 teaspoon chopped thyme
* 1 teaspoon Worcestershire sauce
* ½ small head cauliflower, cut into 1–2-inch (2.5–5 cm) florets
* ½ small head cabbage, cut into 1-inch (2.5 cm) chunks
* Cornstarch (cornflour), for thickening (optional)
* 1 cup (120 g) frozen green peas, thawed

1. In a shallow bowl, combine the flour, sugar, pepper, and salt. Add the beef cubes and toss to coat. Reserve the seasoned flour left over in the bowl.
2. In a large pot or Dutch oven (casserole), heat the olive oil over medium heat. When hot, add the beef cubes in two batches, about 2 minutes per batch. (Don't overcrowd the pot when browning.) Remove the beef cubes to a plate and set aside.
3. To the same pot, add the celery, long carrot pieces, onion, and garlic. Cook until the onion is translucent, about 3 minutes.
4. Meanwhile, in a large measuring cup (jug), combine the stock, wine, vinegar, tomato paste (purée), bay leaves, thyme, Worcestershire sauce, and reserved flour and whisk until smooth. Add to the pot and bring to a simmer, stirring to loosen the caramelized bits at the bottom of the pot.
5. Return the beef to the pot and bring to a simmer. Cover and cook over very low heat until tender, 1½–2 hours, stirring occasionally to prevent the beef from sticking to the bottom of the pan and adding a bit more stock or water if the pot becomes too dry.
6. Add the carrot chunks, cauliflower, and cabbage. Bring to a boil over medium heat, then reduce the heat to low, cover, and simmer until the vegetables are soft, 30–45 minutes. (If the stew is too thin, whisk a tablespoon of cornstarch/cornflour into ¼ cup/2 fl oz/60 ml water or stock and stir into the stew.)
7. Stir the peas into the finished stew, remove from the heat, and let the pot sit for 10 minutes to cook the peas. Season with salt to taste.

Note: The flour forms a layer of starchy coating on the surface of the beef. This seals the moisture and flavor in the beef to make it tender and delicious, and thickens the stew.

→ Pairs with ←
A grain dish and another vegetable or salad dish for a complete meal. It can also serve as a stand-alone light lunch or dinner.

Lamb Masala

Lamb, although a red meat, tends to be produced more naturally on small farms, making it a good substitute for beef if you eat red meat occasionally. Lamb tikka masala involves grilling the meat first before stewing it. Here, I remove that step and use a low-temperature, slow-cooking method to get more flavor from the spices into the meat and make it very tender. Because it takes time, this dish can be scaled up—doubled or tripled. Leftovers can be stored in the refrigerator for one or two days, or in the freezer for a couple of weeks.

Preparation time: 20 minutes, plus overnight marinating time
Cooking time: 3–4 hours
Serves 4
For nut-free, use stock

For the spice paste:
* ¼ teaspoon coriander seeds
* ¼ teaspoon cumin seeds
* ¼ teaspoon fenugreek seeds
* 4 black peppercorns
* 1 green cardamom pod
* 1 bay leaf, dried or fresh
* ½ teaspoon crushed chili flakes, or to taste
* 1-inch piece (15 g) fresh ginger, peeled and crushed with the side of a knife
* 2 cloves garlic, peeled and crushed with the side of a knife

For the lamb:
* 1 teaspoon garam masala
* ½ cup (140 g) yogurt, low-fat (1 percent) or whole-milk
* 1 lb (450 g) boneless lamb leg or shoulder, cut into 1-inch (2.5 cm) cubes

For the stew:
* 2 tablespoons canola (rapeseed) oil
* ½ medium onion, finely chopped
* ½ green bell pepper, finely chopped
* 1 large beefsteak tomato, finely chopped
* 1 tablespoon tomato paste (tomato purée)
* ½ teaspoon fine sea salt
* ½ cup (4 fl oz/120 ml) stock or coconut milk
* 2 tablespoons coarsely chopped cilantro (coriander), for garnish

Make the spice paste:
1. In a mortar and pestle (or spice grinder), grind the coriander seeds, cumin seeds, fenugreek seeds, peppercorns, cardamom, bay leaf, and chili flakes to a fine powder. Add the ginger and garlic and pound into a paste.

Marinate the lamb:
2. In a medium bowl, mix the spice paste, garam masala, and yogurt. Add the lamb and toss to coat in the marinade. Cover and marinate for 2 hours or up to overnight in the refrigerator.

Make the stew:
3. Preheat the oven to 200°F (93°C/Gas Mark ¼) (see *Note*).

4. In a large ovenproof frying pan with a lid or Dutch oven (casserole), heat the oil over medium heat. Add the onion and bell pepper, stir and cook until fragrant, about 1 minute. Add the tomato, tomato paste (purée), and salt. Cook until bubbling. Stir in the stock, add the marinated lamb, and mix well. Bring to a boil, cover, and transfer to the oven.

5. Cook until very tender, at least 3 hours. The longer the lamb cooks, the more tender it becomes.

6. Stir the sauce if it has separated a bit and serve garnished with the chopped cilantro (coriander).

Note: If your oven doesn't go as low as 200°F (93°C/Gas Mark ¼), just cook at the lowest temperature option you have available and check for doneness about 30 minutes earlier.

> ⇒ *Pairs with* ⇐
> A grain dish and 2 vegetable or salad dishes for a complete meal.

Braised Pork Belly with Chestnuts

This slow-cooked pork dish is savory and hearty. Parts of the pork belly can be primarily fat, so choose pieces with a greater proportion of lean—good pork belly cuts should have equal layers of alternating fat and muscle. This dish is rich in collagen from the pork skin, the chestnuts give it a nutty flavor, and the potato thickens the sauce. The initial blanching and rinsing of the pork removes any debris on the surface of the meat and tightens the outside of the pork cubes—resulting in a better flavor and texture. While not a super-healthy dish, it tastes so good and is a great treat once in a while.

Preparation time: 20 minutes
Cooking time: 6 hours 30 minutes
Serves: 4–6

* 2 lb (900 g) pork belly with skin, cut into 2-3-inch (5-7.5 cm) cubes
* 4 tablespoons rice wine
* 2 tablespoons sugar
* 1 tablespoon olive oil
* ½ cup (4 fl oz/120 ml) hot water, plus more as needed
* 1 large onion, sliced
* ¼ cup (25 g) sliced fresh ginger
* 4 cloves garlic, peeled
* 2 star anise
* 2 cardamom pods
* 1 teaspoon fennel seeds
* 2 allspice berries
* 2 bay leaves
* ½ cup (4 fl oz/120 ml) mild lager beer (not too hoppy)
* 1 tablespoon dark soy sauce
* ¼ teaspoon fine sea salt
* 2 teaspoons honey
* 2 cups (260 g) peeled chestnuts (frozen are okay)
* 2 lb (900 g) Yukon Gold potatoes, peeled or unpeeled, cut into 1-inch (2.5 cm) chunks
* 1 scallion (spring onion), finely chopped

1. Preheat the oven to 225°F (107°C/ Gas Mark ¼).

2. In a large pot, combine the pork belly with cold water to cover. Set over high heat and when the water is close to boiling, add 1 tablespoon of the rice wine. Boil rapidly for 2 minutes. Remove the pork and rinse with cold water until clean. Set aside on a plate.

3. In a Dutch oven (casserole) large enough to hold the pork in one snug layer, combine the sugar and olive oil. Set over medium heat and stir until the sugar turns golden brown and starts bubbling. Stir in the hot water to avoid overcaramelization. Remove from the heat.

4. Add the onion, ginger, garlic, star anise, cardamom, fennel seeds, allspice, and bay leaves to the Dutch oven. Lay the pork on top of the spices and add, in the following order: the remaining 3 tablespoons rice wine, the beer, soy sauce, and salt. Spread the honey on the top surface of the pork to prevent it from drying out during cooking.

5. Cover the pot, transfer to the oven, and cook until very tender, about 6 hours.

6. Remove the pork, taking care not to break the cubes apart as they will be very tender by now. Scoop out the whole spices and discard. Add the chestnuts and potatoes to the pan juices. If there isn't enough juice left to cover the chestnuts and potatoes, add additional hot water to cover. Cover and simmer on the stovetop over medium heat until both are cooked through, 10–15 minutes.

7. Plate and top with the pork. Sprinkle the scallion (spring onion) on top.

> → *Pairs with* ←
> A grain dish and 2 vegetable or salad dishes for a complete meal.

Pasta, Noodles & Grains

Whole-Wheat Sourdough Bruschetta

I use whole-wheat sourdough bread instead of regular white bread in this dish. Sourdough is created via fermentation using lactobacillus bacteria in addition to yeast, which is used in the production of traditional white bread. Because of this special fermentation process, sourdough bread is more complex in flavor. Studies show it has a lower glycemic index and lower gluten content than bread fermented by yeast alone. I like to use a skillet to toast the bread since it's faster than using an oven, but you could also use a toaster. Use the highest quality extra-virgin olive oil you have for this dish. It makes a huge difference.

Preparation time: ⑤ minutes
Cooking time: ①⓪ minutes
Serves ④

* 4 slices whole-wheat sourdough bread
* 2 cloves garlic, peeled
* 4 plum tomatoes, ideally San Marzano (or Roma if not available), coarsely chopped
* 2 large fresh basil leaves, sliced into narrow strips
* High-quality extra-virgin olive oil, for drizzling
* Coarse sea salt

1. Heat a cast-iron skillet over medium heat. Put the bread cut-side down in the skillet and toast until crisp and light golden on one side, 3–5 minutes.

2. Remove the toasted bread from the skillet. Rub the garlic on the toasted side of the bread, using it as a grater.

3. Lightly toast the other (ungarlicked) side of the bread in the skillet, about 1 minute. Flip and toast the garlicked side again for 1 minute.

4. To serve, pile the chopped tomatoes on top of the garlicked side of the bread. Sprinkle each with a pinch of coarse sea salt and a few basil strips. Drizzle with olive oil.

> → *Pairs with* ←
> A protein dish and ② vegetable or salad dishes for a complete meal.

Whole-Wheat Pizza
with Mushrooms

My patients want to eat healthier, but at the same time, many still want to enjoy their favorite foods. Pizza is not an unhealthy food per se—it all depends on how it's made. If it is very thick and carbohydrate-heavy, loaded with salt, and drenched in oil, then yes, it's not very healthy, especially if you often eat a large slice. But there are ways to make pizza healthy: thin whole-wheat crust, low-salt, low-fat, and with homemade sauce and high-quality ingredients.

Preparation time: 30 minutes, plus rising time
Cooking time: 25 minutes
Serves 4

For the dough:
* 1 cup (120 g) whole-wheat flour, plus more for kneading
* ½ teaspoon rapid-rise (fast-action) yeast (see *Note 1*)
* ¼ teaspoon sugar
* Pinch of kosher (flaked) salt

For the tomato sauce:
* 2 tablespoons extra-virgin olive oil
* ¼ small onion, chopped
* 1 clove garlic, minced
* ½ teaspoon dried oregano or 1 teaspoon chopped fresh
* ½ teaspoon dried rosemary or 1 teaspoon chopped fresh
* 1 teaspoon chopped basil leaves
* 1 medium heirloom tomato (preferred) or salad tomato, chopped
* ¾ cup (160 g) canned San Marzano tomatoes, chopped
* 1 teaspoon sugar
* ½ teaspoon fine sea salt

For assembly:
* Cornstarch (cornflour), for dusting
* 1 tablespoon extra-virgin olive oil, plus more for drizzling
* 1 cup (100 g) shredded cheese (see *Note 2*)
* ½ cup (45 g) sliced white mushrooms
* Other toppings of your choice (see *Note 3*)
* 1 tablespoon picked basil leaves
* 1 tablespoon arugula (rocket)
* Dash of truffle oil

Make the dough:
1. In a large bowl, combine the flour, yeast, sugar, and salt. Stir in ½ cup (4 fl oz/120 ml) water. Knead in the bowl until smooth and springy, adding more water or flour if needed. The dough should be soft but not sticky. Cover the bowl and set aside until almost doubled in size, 1–1½ hours.

Make the tomato sauce:
2. In a small saucepan, heat the olive oil over medium-low heat. Add the onion, garlic, oregano, rosemary, and basil and cook until fragrant, about 2 minutes. Add the fresh and canned tomatoes and cook over medium heat uncovered until the tomato breaks down, about 10 minutes, stirring from time to time to prevent the sauce from sticking to the bottom of the pan. Stir in the sugar and salt. If you prefer a less chunky sauce, purée the sauce with a handheld blender. Set aside.

Assemble and bake:
3. Preheat the oven to 500°F (260°C/Gas Mark 10). Set a pizza stone or a large cast-iron griddle in the oven to preheat. (A baking sheet would work as well, although the bottom of the pizza may not develop a nice charred crust.)

4. Dust a work surface with flour. Deflate the dough and dust lightly with flour. Roll to a round or rectangle shape as thin as possible without tearing, about ⅛ inch (3 mm) thick. Pull out a piece of foil large enough to hold the pizza and dust lightly with cornstarch (cornflour). Place the rolled-out dough on the foil. (Because the dough is rolled so thin, the foil is used to help transfer the pizza to the stone.)

5. Brush the dough with the olive oil. Spread a thin layer of tomato sauce on top. There should be some areas here and there where you can see the dough through the sauce. Any leftover tomato sauce can be used for extra pizzas, for pasta, or as a dipping sauce.

6. Sprinkle the cheese, mushrooms, and other toppings of choice over the top.

7. Transfer the pizza to the pizza stone or cast-iron griddle. Bake until the edges and some areas of the top are browned, 8–10 minutes. Watch carefully, as it can burn quickly.

8. Let the pizza cool for a few minutes. Top with the basil and arugula (rocket). Drizzle with olive oil and truffle oil. Cut into slices and serve.

Note 1: If you would like to make pizza but don't have the time to let the dough rise, omit the yeast and add 1 teaspoon baking powder to the flour. Mix and knead until the dough comes together in a smooth ball. Proceed with the recipe with no rising time. The crust will be a little more cracker-like and less chewy than traditional pizza dough, but still delicious.

Note 2: At least half of the cheese should be mozzarella—buffalo mozzarella, if you can find it (or a vegetarian alternative). You can use all mozzarella or add some blue, Cheddar, Brie, ricotta, or provolone cheese. You could also make a cheeseless pizza.

Note 3: Topping ideas: olives, capers, sun-dried tomatoes, corn, spinach, artichokes, sliced jalapeño, leeks, sliced zucchini (courgette), or cracked raw eggs.

> ⇥ *Pairs with* ⇤
> A protein dish and 2 vegetable or salad dishes for a complete meal.

Pasta with Clams and Garlic

Clams are a good source of marine protein. Their juices are delicious and will add umami to any dish or soup. Clams filter the water they live in for food, so use those that come from areas with clean water. When buying clams, choose those that are closed or quickly close when tapped, otherwise they should be discarded. If a clam doesn't open after cooking, discard it, too. I use a higher ratio of clams to pasta, to make the dish more savory and to reduce carbohydrates. In Italy, pasta is a small course and served in a portion no more than a small, or at most medium, bowl. A serving of pasta should be no larger than the size of your fist.

Preparation time: ⑤ minutes
Cooking time: ②⓪ minutes
Serves ④

* 8 oz (225 g) linguine
* 3 tablespoons extra-virgin olive oil
* ½ medium onion, chopped
* 4 cloves garlic, minced
* ¼–1 teaspoon crushed chili flakes (optional), to taste
* 20 littleneck clams (about 2 lb/900 g), scrubbed clean (smaller clams are more tender)
* ¼ cup (2 fl oz/60 ml) dry white wine
* 1 tablespoon fresh lemon juice
* 1 cup (60 g) chopped parsley
* Coarse sea salt

1. Bring a large pot of water to a boil for the pasta. Add the linguine and cook until just shy of al dente, 1 minute less than the package directs. Drain.

2. Meanwhile, in a large, deep frying pan with enough room to hold the pasta, heat 2 tablespoons of the olive oil over medium heat. Add the onion, garlic, and chili flakes (if using) and cook until fragrant, about 2 minutes.

3. Add the clams. Stir and add the wine and lemon juice. Cover and cook over medium heat until the clams open, 5–7 minutes. Cook for another 2 minutes, covered.

4. Add the drained pasta and the parsley to the clams, stirring to combine. Cover and cook to blend the flavors, about 1 minute. Season with salt to taste (usually no more than a pinch).

5. Transfer to serving plates and drizzle with the remaining 1 tablespoon olive oil.

→ *Pairs with* ←
② vegetable or salad dishes for a complete meal.

Pasta with Dairy-Free Pesto

Pesto is a very healthy pasta sauce, consisting of olive oil, basil, garlic, and pine nuts. It is rich in plant oil, and I often recommend this as a plant-based, energy-rich dish for those recovering from illness who are trying to gain weight. You can make pesto easily at home with fresher and higher quality ingredients than the store-bought versions, and the result has a brighter, more vibrant taste. Classic recipes call for the use of Parmigiano-Reggiano, but I think it tastes just as good without the cheese. If pine nuts aren't available or you don't like them, macadamia nuts or cashews are a good replacement.

Preparation time: 10 minutes
Cooking time: 15 minutes
Serves 4

* ¼ cup (40 g) pine nuts, or macadamia or cashew nuts
* 2 cloves garlic, crushed with the side of a knife and peeled
* 2 cups (160 g) chopped fresh basil (as fresh as possible, preferably from your own garden)
* ½ teaspoon kosher (flaked) salt
* Dash of fresh lemon juice
* ½ cup (4 fl oz/120 ml) extra-virgin olive oil
* 8 oz (225 g) linguine

1. Bring a large pot of water to a boil for the pasta. Preheat the oven to 350°F (180°C/Gas Mark 4).

2. Arrange the nuts on a baking sheet and toast until slightly fragrant but not browned, about 5 minutes. Remove and let cool.

To make the pesto in a mortar and pestle (my preferred method):

3. Grind the toasted nuts to a coarse paste. Transfer to a large bowl. Pound and grind the garlic to a coarse paste and transfer to the bowl. Finally, pound and grind the basil leaves and salt to a coarse paste and transfer to the bowl. (You may need to do this in two or three batches if the mortar isn't large enough to hold all the basil at once.) Add the lemon juice, then slowly pour in the olive oil, whisking constantly until you have a sauce. The final consistency should be gritty—not too coarse and not too smooth.

To make the pesto in a food processor:

4. In the processor, combine the nuts, garlic, basil, salt, and lemon juice and pulse to chop coarsely. While you pulse the machine, slowly pour in the olive oil.

5. Add the linguine to the boiling water and cook to al dente according to the package directions. Drain and toss with the pesto while the linguine is still hot. Serve immediately.

> ⇀ *Pairs with* ↽
> A protein dish and 2 vegetable or salad dishes for a complete meal.

Steamed Millet and Sofrito Black Beans

This vegan dish combines carbohydrates from a whole grain (millet) and plant protein (black beans). A clinical study found that pairing a grain with beans reduced the spikes in blood sugar level caused by eating the grain. Millet is one of the oldest grains domesticated by humans. Fiber-rich, gluten-free, and full of B vitamins, it can be used in place of rice or wheat berries for variety. It has a nutty fragrance, which I find quite appealing. Millet goes well with strong-flavored ingredients, such as the sofrito black beans here. If you're pressed for time, use a can of black beans, rinsed and drained.

Preparation time: 15 minutes, plus overnight soaking time
Cooking time: 40 minutes–1 hour
Serves 4

For the beans:
* 1 tablespoon extra-virgin olive oil
* ¼ medium onion, chopped
* ¼ teaspoon cumin seeds
* ½ cup (125 g) dried black beans, soaked overnight then drained
* 1 bay leaf
* ¼ teaspoon fine sea salt

For the millet:
* 2 cups (400 g) millet, rinsed and drained

For the sofrito:
* 3 tablespoons extra-virgin olive oil
* 2 cloves garlic, crushed
* ¾ medium onion, chopped
* 1 green bell pepper, diced
* 2 large beefsteak tomatoes, diced
* ½ teaspoon fine sea salt
* 1 jalapeño (optional), or to taste, seeded and chopped
* 1½ cups (50 g) cilantro (coriander) leaves, coarsely chopped, for garnish

Cook the beans:

1. In a small saucepan, heat the olive oil over medium-low heat. Add the onion and cumin seeds and cook until fragrant, about 1 minute. Add the soaked beans, 2 cups (16 fl oz/475 ml) water, the bay leaf, and salt. Bring to a boil, then reduce to a gentle simmer. Cover and cook, stirring occasionally to prevent the beans from sticking to the bottom of the saucepan; after 40 minutes, test doneness by pressing a bean with a fork against the side of the pan. If it can be broken apart, it is done. If not done, continue to cook, checking every 10 minutes or so. Add more water if needed to ensure there is always some water covering the beans. Discard the bay leaf.

Meanwhile, cook the millet:

2. In a medium saucepan, combine the millet and 2½ cups (18 fl oz/550 ml) water. The millet will keep a bit of a bite with this amount of water; if you prefer a softer grain, add ½–1 cup (4–8 fl oz/120–250 ml) more water. Bring to a boil, then reduce to a gentle simmer, cover, and cook until al dente, about 20 minutes. Remove from the heat and set aside.

Make the sofrito:

3. In a frying pan, heat the olive oil over medium-low heat. Add the garlic and onion and cook until translucent, 2–3 minutes. Stir in the bell pepper and cook until the pepper softens, 2–3 minutes. Stir in the tomatoes and simmer over medium-low heat until the tomato breaks down and the mixture becomes saucy, 7–10 minutes. Stir in the salt and jalapeño, if using.

4. To serve, divide the millet among four large bowls or plates, top with the sofrito on one side and black beans on the other, and garnish with the cilantro (coriander).

> → *Pairs with* ←
> A protein dish and 2 vegetable or salad dishes for a complete meal.

Brown Rice with Chanterelle Mushrooms and Leek

Chanterelle mushrooms are a culinary delicacy. They are rich in unique, hard-to-describe flavors and sought after by gourmets. They can be expensive, though not quite as costly as truffles. As such, they are usually used as a flavoring rather than a main ingredient—a little goes a long way. Chanterelle mushrooms are available fresh or dried. If you can't find either form, you can substitute other flavorful mushrooms such as porcini or shiitake. Brown rice has a lower glycemic index than white rice, so is less likely to cause a sugar spike after eating. It also keeps its shape better when cooked, giving it a more chewy "al dente" sensation.

Preparation time: 10 minutes, plus 10 minutes' soaking time if using dried mushrooms
Cooking time: 45 minutes
Serves 4

* ¼ teaspoon saffron threads (optional)
* 2 tablespoons extra-virgin olive oil
* ½ medium onion, chopped
* 2 cloves garlic, minced
* 1 teaspoon fresh oregano or ½ teaspoon dried
* ½ leek, thoroughly cleaned and cut into quarter-lengths (see *Note*, page 111)
* ½ cup (2 oz/60 g) fresh chanterelle mushrooms, cleaned, or ½ oz (15 g) dried, rehydrated (see *Note*)
* 1½ cups (300 g) short-grain brown rice, rinsed
* ½ cup (4 fl oz/120 ml) white wine
* 1 tablespoon apple cider vinegar
* ½ teaspoon fine sea salt, plus extra for seasoning
* ¼ cup (30 g) thawed frozen peas
* 2 tablespoons grated Parmigiano-Reggiano or Manchego cheese, or a vegetarian alternative
* 1 tablespoon chopped parsley, chives, or microgreens, for garnish

1. If using saffron, in a small bowl, soak the saffron in 2 tablespoons of hot water, covered, until needed.

2. In a small saucepan, bring 5 cups (40 fl oz/1.2 liters) water to a bare simmer.

3. In a large saucepan, heat the oil over medium heat. Add the onion and cook until lightly browned, 1–2 minutes. Add the garlic, oregano, leek pieces, and mushrooms and cook until fragrant, about 1 minute.

4. Add the rice and stir to coat with the oil, about 2 minutes. Add the wine, vinegar, and salt. Add 4 cups (32 fl oz/950 ml) of the hot water (if using dried mushrooms, add the soaking water as well). Stir and bring to a boil. Reduce the heat so the liquid is simmering, cover, and cook until the rice is al dente: This should take 20–35 minutes, depending on how chewy you like your grains. If the pan becomes dry as the rice cooks (the rice should stay covered with a thin layer of water), add a little of the remaining hot water.

5. Drizzle the saffron water over the top (if using) and add the peas in a layer. Simmer, uncovered and stirring occasionally, until the peas are cooked through but still brilliant green, 3–5 minutes. Remove from the heat. Stir in the cheese vigorously. Cover and let sit for 5 minutes so the rice can soak up the flavors. Season to taste with salt.

6. Serve garnished with the parsley, chives, or microgreens.

Note: To rehydrate dried chanterelles, soak them in ¼ cup (2 fl oz/60 ml) hot water for 10 minutes. Drain, reserving any soaking water.

> → *Pairs with* ←
> A protein dish and 2 vegetable or salad dishes for a complete meal.

Fried Rice with Eggs and Vegetables

Fried rice can easily be made tasty using lots of oil and salt—but that's not very healthy. Here I use brown rice and millet instead of white rice (which has a higher glycemic index), and less oil than traditional recipes. The ratio of vegetables to rice is also greater than usual, so you're eating fewer carbohydrates. There are mushrooms, sesame oil, and oyster sauce, with optional fish sauce to generate big flavors. You can also cook the grains in a rice cooker.

Preparation time: 20 minutes
Cooking time: 25 minutes
Serves 4

For the rice and millet:
* ½ cup (100 g) short-grain brown rice, rinsed
* ¼ cup (50 g) millet, rinsed

For the scrambled eggs:
* 3 tablespoons olive oil
* ½ cup (45 g) chopped white mushrooms
* 6 eggs
* 5 drops toasted sesame oil
* ⅛ teaspoon coarse sea salt

For the vegetables:
* 1 tablespoon olive oil
* ½ cup (75 g) chopped carrots
* 3 cups (300 g) chopped green vegetables (a combination of bok choy, cucumber, green bell pepper, spinach, or any other green vegetable)
* 1½ tablespoons soy sauce
* ½ tablespoon oyster sauce
* 1 teaspoon fish sauce (optional)
* ½ cup (90 g) chopped tomato
* ¼ cup (25 g) chopped scallions (spring onions)
* 1 teaspoon toasted sesame oil
* 1 clove garlic, minced (optional)
* Coarse sea salt

Cook the rice and millet:

1. In a saucepan, combine the rice and millet with ¾ cup (6 fl oz/175 ml) water. Bring to a boil over medium heat, then reduce to the lowest setting, cover, and simmer until just cooked through, about 15 minutes. This water to grain ratio and cooking time will give you al dente grains, where you can feel each individual grain discretely in your mouth. This is important for the mouthfeel of fried rice. Overcooking will burst the grains open and give you a starchy and mushy fried rice. (If softer rice is preferred, add 25 percent more water and cook for about 20–30 minutes longer.)

2. Once the grains are cooked, spread them on a large baking sheet to cool, and air-dry for 5 minutes or more.

Meanwhile, make the scrambled eggs:

3. In a large frying pan, heat 1 tablespoon of the oil over medium heat. Add the mushrooms and cook until browned, 2–3 minutes. Meanwhile, in a medium bowl, beat the eggs, sesame oil, and salt together. Once the mushrooms are browned, add the remaining oil. Wait 30 seconds, then pour the eggs into the pan. Let them sit, without stirring, until the bottom sets, about 30 seconds, then stir until the eggs are set, 2–3 minutes. Remove to a plate and set aside.

Cook the vegetables:

4. In the same frying pan, heat the oil over medium heat. Add the carrots and cook over medium heat until soft, about 2 minutes. Increase the heat to high. Add the cooled grains and let cook, without stirring, until browned on the underside, about 1 minute. Cook and stir vigorously for 5–7 minutes to heat through and let the grains dry out.

5. Add the green vegetables, soy sauce, oyster sauce, and fish sauce (if using) and stir constantly until the vegetables wilt, 1–2 minutes. Remove from the heat and stir in the scrambled eggs, tomato, scallions (spring onions), sesame oil, and garlic (if using). Mix evenly and season with salt to taste.

> → *Pairs with* ←
> A vegetable or salad dish
> for a complete meal.

Spinach, Pistachio, and Cranberry Quinoa Bowl

Quinoa is a seed from a plant in the amaranth family that grows in the high Andes plateau in Peru and Bolivia. High in protein (14 percent versus 7 percent in rice) and gluten-free, it is also high in minerals and other trace elements (nutrients we need only in minute amounts), such as magnesium, manganese, zinc, and phosphorus. Like buckwheat, it can be used to replace true grains to diversify sources of carbohydrate.

Preparation time: ①⓪ minutes,
plus ①⑤ minutes' soaking time
if using dried cranberries
Cooking time: ②⑤ minutes
Serves ④

* 2 cups (360 g) red quinoa
* 3½ cups (28 fl oz/825 ml) water
  or stock
* ½ cup (75 g) pistachios
* ½ teaspoon olive oil
* 1 teaspoon sugar
* 8 cups (250 g) baby spinach
* ¼ cup (30 g) chopped fresh or
  dried unsweetened cranberries
  (rehydrated by soaking in water
  for 15 minutes and drained)
* 1 tablespoon balsamic vinegar
* ¼ teaspoon coarse sea salt
* Kosher (flaked) salt

1. Preheat the oven to 350°F (180°C/Gas Mark 4).

2. Rinse and drain the quinoa in a fine-mesh sieve. In a large saucepan, combine the quinoa and water and bring to a boil over medium heat. Reduce the heat to low, cover, and simmer until cooked through, about 15 minutes. Remove from the heat, uncover, and let cool. Fluff with a fork and season to taste with kosher (flaked) salt.

3. Meanwhile, in a small bowl, combine the pistachios, olive oil, sugar, and a pinch of kosher salt and toss to coat. Spread on a baking sheet and toast until lightly browned, about 10 minutes. Remove from the oven and let cool.

4. In a large salad bowl. toss together the spinach, cranberries, vinegar, and coarse sea salt.

5. To serve, divide the quinoa among four large shallow bowls or plates. Top with the spinach salad and sprinkle the pistachios over the top.

> → *Pairs with* ←
> A protein dish and a
> vegetable or salad dish for
> a complete meal.

Soba Noodles with Shiitake Mushrooms and Shrimp

This stand-alone dish has a Japanese flavor profile. It has all the major components of a balanced meal—protein, carbohydrates, oil, and vegetables. Take time to bring the ingredients to room temperature before cooking. To keep the shrimp (prawns) tender, it is important they aren't too cold when added to the pan, so they heat up evenly. If they are just out of the refrigerator and still cold inside, the outside may become overcooked while the inside remains uncooked. Do the same for most other ingredients, be it fish or vegetables.

Preparation time: 15 minutes, plus 30 minutes' soaking time if using dried mushrooms
Cooking time: 20 minutes
Serves 4

* 16 large wild shrimp (prawns), peeled and deveined
* 1 lb (450 g) soba noodles
* 6 tablespoons extra-virgin olive oil
* ½ teaspoon kosher (flaked) salt
* 1 tablespoon distilled white vinegar
* 2 teaspoons potato starch or cornstarch (cornflour)
* 6 fresh shiitake mushrooms, stemmed and thinly sliced, or 6 medium dried shiitakes, soaked in water for 30 minutes (or ½ cup/ 45 g sliced white mushrooms if shiitakes are not available)
* 2 scallions (spring onions), finely chopped, whites and green parts kept separate
* 2 teaspoons sugar
* 2 tablespoons sake
* 2 tablespoons soy sauce
* 4 cups (120 g) leafy greens, such as baby spinach or kale, roughly torn, or 6-8 asparagus spears, cut into 1-inch (2.5 cm) pieces

1. Remove the shrimp (prawns) from the refrigerator 15–20 minutes before you're ready to cook.

2. Bring a large pot of water to a boil. Add the soba noodles and cook according to the package directions. Drain and rinse under cold water. Set aside in a sieve.

3. Meanwhile, in a large bowl, combine the shrimp, 2 tablespoons of the oil, the salt, and vinegar and set aside to marinate for 5 minutes.

4. In a large frying pan, heat 2 tablespoons of the oil over medium heat. Remove the shrimp from the marinade, dust with the potato starch and toss well. Add the shrimp to the pan and cook, stirring occasionally, until opaque and cooked through, 2–3 minutes. Transfer the shrimp to a plate.

5. Add the remaining 2 tablespoons oil to the same pan and heat over medium heat. Add the mushrooms and spread in a single layer. Reduce the heat to low, cover, and cook, stirring halfway through, until the mushrooms are softened, about 3 minutes. Add the scallion (spring onion) whites, sugar, sake, and soy sauce. Stir to combine and simmer to bring the sauce together. Add the soba noodles and stir to combine. Stir in the leafy greens and/or asparagus. Cook and let wilt for 1 or 2 minutes.

6. Divide the noodle mixture among four plates and top with the shrimp and scallion greens.

> → *Pairs with* ←
> This serves as a complete, stand-alone meal.

Seafood Paella

Paella is a one-pot dish from Valencia, Spain, and includes the three main categories of nutrients—proteins, carbohydrates, and vegetables. You can improvise with the ingredients in each category to make the dish interesting and different every time you cook it. Traditional paella uses meat—including rabbit, chicken, or duck—and white rice. In this recipe I use shellfish and brown rice, healthier sources of protein and carbohydrates. I also use less rice and more vegetables. Although paella (which means "frying pan" in Spanish) is best cooked in a specialized pan called a paella pan, other large-diameter flat-bottomed pans or pots will do and, in the case of this rendition, are actually more appropriate for the smaller portion size. I prefer my grains on the al dente side, so I have given a range of water quantities and cooking times in case you prefer your grains a little less chewy.

Preparation time: 30 minutes
Cooking time: 50 minutes
Serves 4

* 8 head-on large shrimp (prawns), washed and dried
* 4 tablespoons olive oil
* ¼ cup (2 fl oz/60 ml) white wine
* 1 cup (200 g) short-grain brown rice
* 1 small red onion, chopped
* 1 cup (90 g) sliced white mushrooms
* 2 cloves garlic, minced
* 1 medium tomato, chopped
* 2 red or yellow bell peppers, chopped
* 3½ oz (100 g) parsley, leaves chopped
* 1 teaspoon coarse sea salt
* 1 cup (120 g) fresh or frozen peas, thawed
* A few saffron threads
* 4 mussels (see *Note*), scrubbed
* 4 clams, scrubbed

1. Remove the heads of the shrimp (prawns) and put the heads in a saucepan with 1 tablespoon of the olive oil. Cook over medium heat until fragrant, about 2 minutes. Add the white wine and simmer to combine, about 1 minute. Stir in 1 cup (8 fl oz/250 ml) water and the rice. Set aside for the rice to soak up the flavors in the broth.

2. In a large flat-bottomed pan with a lid, heat the remaining 3 tablespoons olive oil over medium heat. Add the onion, mushrooms, and garlic and cook until fragrant, about 1 minute. Add the tomato, bell peppers, parsley, and salt. Cover and cook over medium heat until softened, about 5 minutes.

3. Remove the shrimp heads from the saucepan containing the rice and discard them. Add the rice and broth to the large pan along with the peas and saffron. (If you prefer less chewy grains, add an additional ½ cup/4 fl oz/120 ml water here.) Stir to combine, then even out the surface and bring to a boil over medium heat. Reduce the heat to a simmer, cover, and cook over low heat until the rice is cooked through to your liking, 20–35 minutes.

4. While the rice cooks, peel and devein the shrimp.

5. Around 5 minutes before the end of the cooking time, uncover the pan, press the mussels and clams into the rice, hinge-sides down. Place the shrimp in a single layer on top of the rice. Cover and cook over medium heat until the mussels and clams open (discard any that don't open) and the shrimp is cooked through, about 5 minutes.

Note: Chances are you cannot buy just 4 mussels, so steam any extras following the directions on page 190.

> → *Pairs with* ←
> This can serve as a stand-alone meal, or pairs with a vegetable or salad dish for extra vegetables.

Desserts

Fruit Salad

Instead of cakes, cookies, and pastries, I like to serve fruit as a dessert. Fruits contain less sugar, and that sugar is bound to the fibers, so is less likely to cause a spike in blood sugar. Try to buy fruits of different colors, which will give your body the variety of micronutrients it needs. Avoid canned fruits, fruit juices, or syrups, all of which are high in sugar.

Preparation time: ①⑤ minutes
Serves ②
For nut-free, dairy-free, and vegan, choose an appropriate flavour option

* 1 cup (120–150 g) chopped yellow/gold fruits, such as apricots, cantaloupe melon, oranges and other citrus, mango, papaya, or peaches
* 1 cup (120–150 g) chopped red or green fruits, such as kiwifruits, honeydew melon, green apples, pears, strawberries, raspberries, pomegranate seeds, red apples, or cherries
* 1 cup (120–150 g) chopped dark or white fruit, such as blueberries, blackberries, figs, bananas, or dragon fruit
* Your choice of flavor boost (optional; see *Flavor options*)

1. Combine all the chopped fruits in a serving bowl. If desired, top with your chosen flavor boost.

Flavor options

1 tablespoon espresso + 1 tablespoon half-and-half (single cream)

1 tablespoon sherry or Madeira + 1 tablespoon crushed pistachios

1 tablespoon honey + a dusting of ground cinnamon

1 tablespoon unsweetened coconut flakes + 1 tablespoon finely chopped dark chocolate

1 teaspoon matcha powder + 1 tablespoon crushed chocolate wafer cookies

1 tablespoon chopped fresh mint + 1 teaspoon grated lemon zest

Blueberry Oat Crumble

This crumble uses oats and berries, without adding a lot of refined carbohydrates or sugar, to create a healthy and delicious dessert. If you want to reduce the carbohydrates even more, you can use chickpea (gram) flour instead of whole-wheat flour, which also makes this dessert gluten-free. Blueberries can be replaced by other colorful berries, such as raspberries or blackberries, or even kiwi. I also use honey, as it contains more micronutrients, however, fructose and glucose in honey are still simple sugars, so should be limited to less than 10 grams per meal; this recipe contains about 5 grams per serving.

Preparation time: 10 minutes
Cooking time: 30 minutes
Serves 4
For gluten-free, use chickpea (gram) flour

For the filling:
* 2 cups (300 g) fresh blueberries or thawed frozen blueberries
* 1 teaspoon honey dissolved in 2 tablespoons water
* 1–3 teaspoons cornstarch (cornflour)
* Pinch of fine sea salt

For the topping:
* ¾ cup (70 g) old-fashioned rolled oats
* ¼ cup (35 g) whole-wheat flour or chickpea (gram) flour
* 1 tablespoon honey dissolved in 4 tablespoons water
* 1 tablespoon coconut oil, melted
* Pinch of fine sea salt

1. Preheat the oven to 375°F (190°C/ Gas Mark 5).

Make the filling:
2. In a 6-inch (15 cm) round baking dish, toss the blueberries, honey mixture, cornstarch (cornflour) and salt, using less cornstarch, about 1 teaspoon, with fresh berries and 2–3 teaspoons with frozen berries. Mix well to combine and even out the surface.

Make the topping:
3. In a large bowl, combine the oats, flour, honey mixture, coconut oil, and salt and toss until just combined. Crumble evenly over the top of the filling.

4. Bake until the top is light golden brown and the filling is bubbling, 25–30 minutes. Let cool and serve.

Kiwi and Honeydew Sorbet with Cashew Milk

I typically look for dessert options other than ice cream, because of its cold temperature and high sugar content. Cold desserts chill the stomach, impeding digestive functions when you need them the most, after a meal. On those occasions when you really do want a cold dessert, eat this low-sugar, dairy-free fruit sorbet. You can replace the kiwi and melon with almost any other fruits, such as mangoes, raspberries, or peaches. You can also use frozen fruits.

Preparation time: ①⓪ minutes,
plus ① hour freezing time
Serves ④

* 4 kiwifruits, peeled and cut in half
* 1 lb (450 g) honeydew melon, peeled and cut into ½-inch (1.25 cm) pieces
* 1 tablespoon honey
* 4 tablespoons unsweetened cashew milk
* 4 dashes of triple sec liqueur (optional)

1. Arrange the fruit chunks on a baking sheet and freeze until solid, at least 1 hour.

2. Meanwhile, chill a blender jar or the bowl of a food processor. (If you have a blender with a very narrow base, the food processor may be a better option here.)

3. Put the frozen fruits and honey in the chilled blender or food processor. Pulse until the fruit is in tiny crystals and is light and fluffy.

4. Divide among four glasses. Drizzle 1 tablespoon of cashew milk and a dash of triple sec (if using) over each serving.

Mango Lassi

Mango contains digestive enzymes, and when eaten at the end of a meal, this dessert aids digestion, making it a better choice than cake or ice cream. There are several modifications to this recipe that make it healthier than the traditional version. I've added turmeric, reduced the ratio of dairy product, and used honey instead of sugar. Turmeric has anti-inflammatory properties, but it needs to be blended with lipids to be absorbed efficiently by the body. Here, the high-speed blending in the presence of kefir/yogurt will achieve that. Yogurt and kefir are fermented milk products, rich in probiotics. Kefir has both lactobacilli and saccharomyces (yeast). Yogurt usually has lactobacilli and streptococci. I suggest alternating kefir and yogurt from day to day, to get a more diverse probiotic mixture, or do a 50/50 mix of yogurt and kefir. Be sure to use "live culture" kefir or yogurt. Since I reduced the amount of dairy in this recipe, I added banana to make up for the reduced thickness in consistency.

Preparation time: 10 minutes
Serves 4

* 4 fully ripe mangoes (about 10 oz/280 g each), chopped (see *Note*)
* 1 ripe banana, sliced
* 2 cups (560 g) live-culture kefir or yogurt
* 2 tablespoons honey
* 1 teaspoon ground turmeric
* Pinch each of ground cinnamon and cardamom (optional)
* 4 mint sprigs and a few pomegranate seeds (optional), for garnish

1. In a blender, combine the mangoes, banana, kefir, 2 cups (16 fl oz/475 ml) water, the honey, turmeric, and cinnamon/cardamom (if using) and blend on high until very smooth.

2. Divide among four glasses. If desired, garnish with mint and pomegranate seeds. Serve immediately.

Note: Use fully ripened mangoes that are soft and sweet. If the mangoes are firm, leave on the countertop for a few days to ripen them fully. There are several cultivars (subtypes) of mango. Find one that is sweeter and has fewer fibers. Frozen mangoes are fine, but canned mango with syrup has too much sugar.

Chocolate-Filled Raspberries

Chocolate together with low-sugar fruits is a healthy replacement for richer chocolate desserts. Dark chocolate (70–85 percent cacao) is preferred for its lower sugar content. All berries, with the exception of blueberries, are low-sugar fruits, containing about 5 percent sugar. The creamy mouthfeel and slightly bitter taste of chocolate combined with the succulent mild sweetness of berries such as raspberries or strawberries creates a satisfying dessert. I use a hot-water bath to melt the chocolate, as using a stove burner or microwave runs the risk of overheating or burning. Note the small portion of the dessert: Dessert is to complement and finish a meal, not to fill up a gap and make you feel full.

Preparation time: 25 minutes
Serves 4

* ⅓ cup (60 g) chopped dark chocolate or dark chocolate chips/chunks
* 1 cup (130 g) raspberries

1. Put the chocolate in a small zip-top plastic bag. Squeeze out the air and seal the bag. Submerge the bag in a covered bowl or saucepan with very warm water, 120°–140°F (50°–60°C). The temperature should be such that you can touch it but not hold your hand in it for too long. (Or use an instant-read thermometer if you have one.) The chocolate should melt in 5–10 minutes. Gently squeeze the bag until smooth.

2. Line up the raspberries, open-side up, on a tray. Cut a very small hole in a lower corner of the bag. Fill each raspberry with chocolate. Let set either at room temperature or in the refrigerator for 10–15 minutes.

Note: Some people are concerned about the sugar content in chocolate. Eating chocolate is fine—depending on how much sugar is in the chocolate and how much you eat. For example, a 1-inch (2.5 cm) square piece of dark chocolate weighs a little over ½ ounce (15 g) and contains only about 5 grams of sugar, if it is 70 percent cacao, or 3 grams if 80 percent cacao. This isn't enough to make any significant change in blood glucose level. On the other hand, most individually wrapped, single-serving chocolate bars have between 20 and 40 grams of sugar. Read the product label and aim at less than 10 grams of sugar per serving. This translates to two square pieces of dark chocolate or half or one-quarter of a "single-serving" chocolate bar.

Flourless Cookies with Pumpkin and Sunflower Seeds

This dessert is made from seeds and uses no flour. Fat from seeds is healthy fat, and flax contains a lot of omega-3 fatty acids, an anti-inflammatory substance. With all the nutty flavors harmonized by coconut oil—another healthy fat—this dish serves as a low-sugar (7 grams per serving) dessert. This recipe can easily be scaled up, and the cookies can be stored in a sealed container at room temperature for a few days.

Preparation time: 5 minutes
Cooking time: 25 minutes
Makes: 8 cookies

* ¾ cup (105 g) hulled pumpkin seeds
* ¼ cup (35 g) sesame seeds
* ¼ cup (35 g) ground flaxseeds
* 1 teaspoon cornstarch (cornflour)
* 2 tablespoons natural brown sugar, such as turbinado
* ¼ cup (70 g) sunflower seed butter or creamy peanut butter
* 1 teaspoon coconut oil

1. Preheat the oven to 350°F (180°C/Gas Mark 4). Line a baking sheet with parchment paper.

2. Spread the pumpkin seeds and sesame seeds in a single layer on the lined baking sheet and toast until golden, 7–10 minutes. Remove and let cool. Leave the oven on and reduce the temperature to 300°F (150°C/Gas Mark 2). Keep the lined baking sheet on hand.

3. In a medium bowl, toss together the pumpkin seeds, sesame seeds, ground flaxseeds, cornstarch (cornflour), and brown sugar. Add the sunflower seed butter, coconut oil, and 2 tablespoons water. Mix and knead with a spoon until well combined.

4. Scoop up a heaping tablespoonful of the mixture and form into a ball. Place the ball on the lined baking sheet. With the back of a spoon or your hand, press the ball into a 2-inch (5 cm) disc about ¼ inch (6 mm) thick. Repeat with the remaining dough to make about eight cookies.

5. Transfer to the oven and bake until set and lightly golden, about 15 minutes. (If the cookies are still not done, continue to bake and check every few minutes.) Let cool on the baking sheet.

Sticky Rice and Bean Cake with Jujube Dates and Pine Nuts

Purple sweet glutinous rice, also called black sweet rice or black glutinous rice, gives this dish a unique sticky texture. Although it is called "glutinous" rice, it contains no gluten. Red adzuki beans, rich in protein and fiber, help to lower the glycemic index of the dish. Jujube dates nurture digestive functions and improve fatigue. The white and fragrant pine nut garnish is a lovely contrast to the intense dark red color of this dish.

Preparation time: 15 minutes, plus overnight soaking time
Cooking time: 1 hour
Serves 4

* ½ cup (100 g) purple or white sticky rice, rinsed and drained
* ¼ cup (50 g) dried adzuki beans or black beans, soaked overnight at room temperature, rinsed, and drained
* 8 dried jujube dates, whole or halved (or 4 fresh or dried figs if not available)
* ¼ cup (40 g) dark raisins or golden raisins (sultanas)
* 1 tablespoon sugar
* Pinch of fine sea salt
* 1 tablespoon canola (rapeseed) oil
* 2 tablespoons pine nuts

1. In a small saucepan, combine the drained rice and beans (which should come to about 1 cup in total volume) with the jujubes, raisins, sugar, salt, and 1 cup (8 fl oz/250 ml) water. Bring to a boil, then reduce to a gentle simmer, cover, and cook until the beans are tender, 20–30 minutes (if not sure, taste a bean). There should always be some water covering the mixture as it cooks; if there isn't, add a little.

2. Once the beans are tender, uncover and simmer to evaporate any extra liquid in the pan. Let cool until warm, 10–15 minutes.

3. Brush four small bowls with a dash of canola (rapeseed) oil to prevent the rice from sticking. Fill each bowl with cooked rice and beans and flatten the top, then steam for 5 minutes (see *Note*).

4. Invert the bowls onto plates and remove the bowl to reveal round cakes. Top with pine nuts.

Note: Steaming the rice and beans makes them taste even better and gives them a more "sticky" mouthfeel.

Variation: At the end of Step 2, instead of steaming, divide the mixture among four bowls and top with the pine nuts to serve.

Sample Menus

Designed for people who don't have much time to spend on cooking lunch, these menus take advantage of some of the dishes that can be cooked for dinner, with leftovers used for breakfast and lunch the next day, to save time. Otherwise, a "30 minutes or less" lunch can be prepared in the morning. Each lunch and dinner should finish with some fruit, if the portion of vegetables is not equal to the sum of the proteins and carbohydrates.

	Breakfast	Lunch	Dinner
Monday	* Oatmeal with Fruit and Nuts * Scrambled Eggs with Mushrooms * Red Cabbage Coleslaw * An apple	* Whole-wheat dinner roll * Lentil Dal * Shakshuka with Okra and Tomatoes	* Honey Glazed Mahi-mahi with Parsley * Pasta with Clams and Garlic * Caesar Salad
Tuesday	* Granola with Mixed Seeds and Grains * Boiled Egg * A bowl of berries	* Tabbouleh * Honey Glazed Mahi-mahi with Parsley (leftover) * Fennel Salad with Fruit and Nuts	* Cannellini Bean Soup * Steamed Squash with Nuts and Basil * Assorted Vegetables with Baba Ghanoush
Wednesday	* Yogurt Cup with Mixed Berries and Nuts * Chia Seed Pudding * Green Smoothie * Assorted Vegetables with Baba Ghanoush (leftover)	* Chickpeas with Farro, Parsley, Cucumber and Tomato * Cannellini Bean Soup (leftover)	* Monkfish Stew with Red Sauce * Whole-Wheat Sourdough Bruschetta * Braised Leeks with Thyme
Thursday	* Millet Porridge * Silky Tofu with Dashi and Soy Sauce * 2 servings of fruit	* Monkfish Stew with Red Sauce (leftover) * Full Spectrum Salad * A slice of multigrain bread	* Lima Bean Chili with Green Beans * Cauliflower, Mushroom, and Sauerkraut Casserole
Friday	* Nut-Butter Multigrain Toast with Poached Fruits * Lima Bean Chili with Green Beans (leftover) * Red Smoothie	* Cauliflower, Mushroom and Sauerkraut Casserole (leftover) * Red Cabbage Coleslaw * 2 Boiled Eggs	* Steamed Whole Branzino with Scallions and Ginger * Baby Bok Choy Braised with Oyster Sauce * Peruvian Stuffed Peppers
Saturday	* Oatmeal with Fruit and Nuts * Peruvian Stuffed Peppers (leftover) * 2 servings of fruit	* Lemon-Garlic Baked Cod * Chunky Cucumber Salad with Tomato and Feta * A slice of whole-wheat sourdough toast	* Pan-Seared Sea Bass * Pasta with Dairy-free Pesto * Roasted Brussels Sprouts with Rosemary
Sunday	* Kasha * Green Pea Purée with Tomatoes and Cauliflower * Pan-Fried Asparagus	* Tuna Steak with Cucumber and Carrot Ribbons * Sautéed Zucchini with Garlic * Cannellini Bean Soup	* Soba Noodles with Shiitake Mushrooms and Shrimp * Seaweed Salad with Miso and Sesame Seeds

	Breakfast	Lunch	Dinner
Monday	* Whole-Wheat Pancakes * Poached Egg * Yellow Smoothie * A bowl of berries	* Aioli Shrimp with Walnuts * Guacamole Salad * Peppery Collard Greens with Tomato and Jalapeño	* Steamed Millet and Sofrito Black Beans * Vegetables and Tofu with Herbs En Papillote * Steamed Kabocha Squash Bowl
Tuesday	* Avocado Toast with Toppings * Chia Seed Pudding * An orange and a peach	* Steamed Millet and Sofrito Black Beans (leftover) * Watercress Salad with Clementines and Wild Rice	* Turkey Meatballs with Tomato Sauce * Tabbouleh * Roasted Brussels Sprouts with Rosemary
Wednesday	* Almond Milk Vegan Protein Shake * Tabbouleh (leftover) * 2 servings of mixed berries	* Turkey Meatballs with Tomato Sauce (leftover) * Full Spectrum Salad * A bowl of brown rice	* Fried Rice with Eggs and Vegetables * Simmered Daikon Radish and Shiitake Mushrooms * Salt and Vinegar Napa Cabbage
Thursday	* Boiled Sweet Potato with Refried Beans * Fruit Salad	* Fried Rice with Eggs and Vegetables (leftover) * Braised Leeks with Thyme * Silky Tofu with Dashi and Soy Sauce	* Kimchi Tofu Stew * Salt and Vinegar Broiled Spanish Mackerel * Baby Bok Choy Braised with Oyster Sauce
Friday	* Kasha * Steamed Egg Custard * Radish, Cucumber and Dill Salad with Sour Cream	* Kimchi Tofu Stew (leftover) * Peppery Collard Greens with Tomato and Jalapeño * Kasha (leftover)	* Spinach, Pistachio, and Cranberry Quinoa Bowl * Roasted Beet and Radicchio Salad with Pine Nuts * Pan-Fried Asparagus
Saturday	* Millet Porridge * Fava Beans with Porcini Mushrooms and Sun-Dried Tomatoes * A serving of fruit	* Pil-Pil Haddock * Whole-Wheat Sourdough Bruschetta * Sautéed Zucchini with Garlic * Arugula Salad with Walnuts and Shrimp	* Seared Scallops * Green Pea Purée with Tomatoes and Cauliflower * Roasted Butternut Squash Soup
Sunday	* Yogurt Cup with Mixed Berries and Nuts * Red Smoothie * Fruit Salad	* Vegan Tempeh Burger * Edamame with Roasted Cauliflower Steaks	* Seafood Paella * Radish, Cucumber, and Dill Salad with Sour Cream

Index

Author Acknowledgments

First and foremost, I would like to thank all my patients who motivated me to write this book. Their courage, perseverance, and grace when fighting a serious illness have always been an inspiration to me. Many patients specifically asked me to write a book like this, to help them implement what we discussed about how to improve their health. Without their prompting and encouragement, this book would not have gotten started.

I am also indebted to many mentors and colleagues along the way in my scientific and medical careers, as without them I would not have the experience and expertise to write this health-oriented cookbook. There are too many to name all of them individually. Among them, the late Eckhard Podack, MD, PhD, who taught me not only the essence of science and an honorable work ethic, but also how to create a good life experience from small, everyday things, including good foods. That planted the seeds of my appreciation of the culinary arts and sciences. Also the late Herbert Fred, MD, who had the most profound influence on how I practice medicine. When he trained us, he always prodded us to look beyond the medical pathology and go one step deeper in a patient's life for the real "diagnosis." For example, when we presented a case of a patient and said, "The problem is shortness of breath and the diagnosis is congestive heart failure," he would say, "No, the problem is congestive heart failure, the diagnosis is the patient ate too much salt." Those insightful teachings made me take a holistic approach when caring for a patient, including looking closely at their diet and lifestyle to practice integrative medicine.

Special thanks to Debra Black for your support in bringing this book into being. I am grateful to the outstanding team at Phaidon. Thank you Emily Takoudes, Executive Commissioning Editor, for brainstorming together and advising on the ideas, theme, and structure of the book that would make it useful and accessible to global readers and home cooks. You guided me in every step it takes to convert an idea into a book we can hold in our hands. Thank you Amy Stevenson, the Development Editor who worked closely with me, for your patience and diligence in getting the contents into shape and your handholding of a rookie cookbook writer. Thank you Rachel Malig, Project Editor, for the meticulous work in bookmaking and refining the content; to Kate Slate for her attention to detail with the text; to Marwan Kaabour for his wonderful design; and to Luke Albert for his stunning food photography. It was a privilege working with you all.

I offer my appreciation to many friends who have shared their insights, techniques, and tips in cooking home meals, to guests who have sat at my dining table—all offering feedback, suggestions, and encouragement so I continue to improve my cooking, and to culinary teachers from whom I have learned over the years.

Lastly, I conclude this book in deep gratitude to my family, Maya and Adrian. I am blessed to have you in my life. It is for you that I put my heart into preparing everyday meals. Thank you, Maya, for being the greatest cheerleader for this endeavor and for your support when the going gets tough. Thank you, Adrian, for being an unsuspecting test subject, who, despite your tender age, has a discerning palate and was able to point out the major ingredients in the foods I prepared, including the most important one: "Daddy, I think it has cauliflower, olive oil, salt, and... love."

About the Author

Dr. Gary Deng is the Medical Director of Integrative Medicine at Memorial Sloan Kettering Cancer Center (MSKCC) and Clinical Professor of Medicine at Weill Cornell Medical College of Cornell University in New York City. Dr. Deng's professional expertise is patient-centered holistic supportive care for cancer patients. He aims to improve patient experience and quality of life, optimize their internal and external environments, strengthen their physical and mental resilience, enhance treatment outcome, speed up recovery, and reduce risk of disease recurrence and complications—all so they can achieve optimal health and wellness.

Dr. Deng received his medical degree from Beijing Medical University, and his PhD in Microbiology and Immunology from University of Miami School of Medicine. He completed his clinical training at the University of Texas Medical School at Houston, and his research training at the University of Texas M.D. Anderson Cancer Center. Since 2003, he has built a robust integrative physician practice, which has become a highly utilized and trusted resource for the Cancer Center. He has taken a leadership role in the emerging and evolving field of integrative oncology, and is active in conducting research and developing innovations in the field, including: nutritional plans, botanical agents, yoga, and acupuncture.

Dr. Deng is a keen home cook and has crafted the recipes in this book from his own experience of cooking delicious, nutritious food within the time constraints of his busy work schedule.

Recipe Notes

* Eggs are always large (US)/medium (UK).

* Herbs, unless indicated otherwise, are always fresh, and parsley is always flat-leaf.

* Individual vegetables and fruits, such as carrots and apples, are assumed to be medium, unless otherwise specified.

* When no quantity is specified, for example of oils, salts, and herbs used for finishing dishes, quantities are discretionary and flexible.

* Exercise caution when making fermented products, ensuring all equipment is spotlessly clean, and seek expert advice if in any doubt.

* Exercise a high level of caution when following recipes involving any potentially hazardous activity, including the use of high temperatures, open flames and when deep-frying.

* Some recipes include raw or lightly cooked eggs and fish, and fermented products. These should be avoided by the elderly, infants, and pregnant women; convalescents and anyone with an impaired immune system should exercise caution.

* Cooking and preparation times are for guidance only, as individual ovens vary. If using a convection (fan) oven, follow the manufacturer's instructions concerning oven temperatures.

* Both imperial and metric measures are used in this book. Follow one set of measurements throughout, not a mixture, as they are not interchangeable.

* All spoon and cup measurements are level, unless otherwise stated. 1 teaspoon = 5 ml; 1 tablespoon = 15 ml. Australian standard tablespoons are 20 ml, so Australian readers are advised to use 3 teaspoons in place of 1 tablespoon when measuring small quantities.

Phaidon Press Limited
2 Cooperage Yard
Stratford
London E15 2QR

Phaidon Press Inc.
65 Bleecker Street
New York NY 10012

phaidon.com

First published 2022
© 2022 Phaidon Press Limited

ISBN 978 1 83866 475 6

A CIP catalogue record for this book is available from the British Library and the Library of Congress.

Commissioning Editor: Emily Takoudes
Project Editor: Rachel Malig
Production Controller: Lily Rodgers
Design (interior): Marwan Kaabour
Cover Design: Phaidon
Photography: Luke Albert
Author Photograph (page 255): Stephen Cardone
 at NY Headshots

Printed in China

The publisher would like to thank Deborah Aaronson, Evelyn Battaglia, Julia Hasting, João Mota, Elizabeth Parson, Libby Silbermann, Kate Slate, Ellie Smith, Amy Stevenson, and Emilia Terragni for their contributions to the book.